Twenty-Four Hundred

Tennessee Pensioners

Revolution
&
War *of* 1812

Compiled By:
Zella Armstrong

Southern Historical Press, Inc.
Greenville, South Carolina

Originally printed 1937 by:
Zella Armstrong

New Material Copyright 2022 to:
Southern Historical Press, Inc.

SOUTHERN HISTORICAL PRESS, INC.
PO BOX 1267
Greenville, SC   29601

ISBN #978-1-63914-090-9

Printed in the United States of America

To one whose gifts of mind and heart are ever at the service of his State,

Who has contributed more than any other of his century to the preservation of pioneer history,

Whose precept and example continually encourage research in and record of the story of Tennessee,

Who deserves a Citation of Merit and a Medal of Honor from the State which acclaims him—Citizen,

TO JUDGE SAMUEL COLE WILLIAMS

*This Roll of Tennessee's Soldier Sons
is Dedicated*

In reading the names of men who served in the Revolution and drew pension for that service it should be borne in mind that hundreds who did not draw pension fought literally for and in Tennessee.

FOREWORD

When men in the Tennessee country during the years of the Revolution volunteered to follow Shelby or Sevier from love of adventure, patriotic instinct, or the urge to protect their homes, they frequently returned to those homes without pay and without formal enrollment in any definite organization. John Sevier's following was a fluid group, changing as the campaigns changed. The seat of government in North Carolina was far away, communication was difficult and even when reports were made they did not always reach the capital of the state. Many men rescued women and children from marauding Indians without thought of recompense or credit; many were killed in the effort to save cabins and stations. In hundreds of cases their names are not known.

Every man in the mountains answered the call to assemble at Sycamore Shoals to join Shelby and Sevier for the march to the battle which became famous as King's Mountain and a draft had to be held, not to determine which men should go to war but who should stay at home to protect the women and children.[1] Unfortunately the result of that draft was not preserved; but men who were appointed for home duty had revolutionary service equally with those who marched to King's Mountain.

For all these reasons it is impossible to assemble a complete list of men who served in the Tennessee country in the Revolution.

Thousands of veterans from other states moved to the new country when Tennessee was erected and later hundreds of them were granted pensions. As will be seen they had served in New York, New Jersey, Connecticut, Massachusetts, Pennsylvania, Virginia, South Carolina, Delaware, Maryland, Georgia and North Carolina. The North Carolina list includes men who had resided in what is now Tennessee during the Revolution as well as men who moved to Tennessee from points which are still in North Carolina.

Thus eleven of the original thirteen states are represented in the Tennessee revolutionary pension list.

The War of 1812 pensioners are, however, almost without exception Tennesseeans.

Lists of soldiers who received pension under the several Pension Acts were published by Act of Congress. The pensioners who were living in 1840 were listed in the Census of that year and their names were published.

In the lists the names are arranged by counties and not then always alphabetically, thus making research extremely difficult and tedious even if the researcher should have access to all the government lists which can happen in few libraries as they are practically out of print.

Some veterans applied for and received pensions and died between

---

[1]*Annals of Tennessee,* Dr. J. G. M. Ramsey, page 228.

the dates of published lists and therefore appear in none. Some applied after 1840. Many widows applied after 1840. These names when known have been included in the following list.

The names are printed here as they appear in the Government publications although it is evident that the printers had difficulty in deciphering copy. Sometimes the name of a soldier is spelled in as many ways as there are lists and only residence, service, age, and approximate sound of the name indicate that the soldier is one and the same. For instance "McAdow" is evidently the name familiar to us as "Mc-Adoo." The name "Marsha Green" is not quite so easily identified with "Meshack Greer," although there can be no doubt that they are the same. Clerks in pension offices followed a phonetic system which is sometimes puzzling and evidently the result of their conclusion when transmitted to Washington in long hand was not entirely clear to the authorities in some instances at least.

Each of the variations in spelling is included in the following list without attempt to correct or modernize with one or two exceptions when the deviation is flagrant. For instance Naomi Sevier, widow of Valentine Sevier, is Nasmi Sevier in the Government publications. The name is printed correctly in this list.

In compiling this roll information given on every list was assembled. If the pensioner lived through the period from 1816 to 1840 his name appears perhaps on three or four lists, but it is printed here but once.

The majority of the soldiers in the following list were veterans of the Revolution. War of 1812 service is indicated by "1812" in parenthesis when the fact was personally known to the compiler or is indicated in the text as service in Tennessee troops or U. S. troops, neither of these phrases being possible for Revolutionary service. The age of the pensioner is also a factor in determining service as men of sixty years or less in 1840 could not have served in the Revolution. They were therefore in the War of 1812, the Indian campaigns or in rare cases invalid dependents of soldiers.

It is interesting that only two fraudulent applications were made and granted. These two pensions were stopped as it was proved that the men did not serve in the Revolution.

The words "dropped from the roll," which frequently appear in the Government lists, have a very different significance. After the first pension act, very rigid requirements were instituted. Some of the original pensioners refused to accede to these requirements feeling that they were humiliated by them and the protesting pensioners were "dropped from the roll." In almost every case they were restored later, if they had survived, when the rigorous requirements were abated.

Another point which should be explained to the genealogical researcher or the amateur indulging in the game of ancestor hunting is the fact that some pensioners drew pension in different counties in Tennessee in different years without removal from their original dwelling sites although others did move from one county to another. A knowledge of Tennessee county history makes the matter clear in some cases while others are puzzling. If both counties mentioned are in East Tennessee or Middle Tennessee it is probable that the soldier resided in a section which was cut off for the erection of a new county as population increased. If one county is in the East and one in the West the soldier probably moved. Thus a veteran might have lived in Rhea County in 1818 and in Hamilton in 1840 without a change of residence; but if he lived in Knox County in 1818 and in Shelby in 1840 he had moved or the name is that of another soldier.

In compiling this list and the accompanying data erection of the counties was carefully considered. Each veteran who drew pension in two counties has but one entry when it is clear that the second county residence was in a section cut off from an older county, but in each case both counties are given. When the circumstances are not entirely clear the name is inserted twice lest some pensioner be omitted.

Many widows applied for pension who were unable to prove marriage. Proof of the marriage ceremony was requisite and the authorities had no choice but to disallow claims when it could not be given. The marriages had taken place frequently in a period of excitement and confusion, the revolutionary years; sometimes no records were made and sometimes all records were burned. Often the officiating clergymen or squires as well as all witnesses had passed away. In these disallowed claims there is no evidence of misrepresentation and there is valuable genealogical information as each widow, in support of her claim, gave all possible data of parentage, children, children's birth and marriages and in some instances even the names of grandchildren.

Information for the roll of Tennessee Pensioners, Revolution and War of 1812, which follows was compiled and collated from the published Government lists commonly called the list of 1816, the list of 1818, the list of 1828, the list of 1832, the Census of 1840, the list of the heirs of non-commissioned officers killed in service (War of 1812), the manuscript record of the Knoxville Agency (by courtesy of the McClung Collection, Lawson McGhee Library, Knoxville), Blount County records, furnished by W. E. Parham, and other county records.

ZELLA ARMSTRONG.

Chattanooga, Tennessee.
May 1, 1937.

LIST OF PENSIONERS

Abbott, John; 1818 list age 70; served in N C line; drew pension in Grainger Co; d May 10 1828.

Abernathy, David; 1832 list age 75; served in N C line; drew pension in Giles Co.

Acilla, see John A Honey; 1818 list age 74; served in A W White's regt; drew pension in Claiborne Co.

Acor, Jacob; 1818 list age 74; served in Conn line; drew pension in Washington Co; d June 18 1833.

Acree, Cronamus; 1818 list age 87; served in Md line; drew pension in Roane Co.

Acree, James; 1818 list age 78; also 1840 Census; served in Va line; drew pension in 1832 in Knox Co; drew pension in 1840 in Roane Co.

Acree, John; 1832 list age 74; served in Va line; drew pension in Sullivan Co.

Adams, Jesse; drew pension in Nashville Agency.

Adams, John; 1832 list age 75; served in Va line; drew pension in Montgomery Co.

Adams, Micajah; 1832 list age 75; also 1840 Census; served in Va mil; drew pension in Sullivan Co.

Adcock, John; 1818 list age 79; served in Va line; drew pension in Davidson Co.

Adcock, John C; drew pension in Nashville Agency.

Adcock, Thomas; 1832 list age 73; served in N C line; drew pension in Morgan Co.

Ailsworth, George; 1818 list age 76; also 1840 Census; served in Va troops; drew pension in White Co.

Akin, James; 1832 list age 74; also 1840 Census; served in N C line; drew pension in Roane Co.

Alberton, Early; 1832 list age 78; served in N C mil; drew pension in Overton Co.

Alexander, Charles; drew pension in Nashville Agency.

Alexander, Dan; 1832 list age 70; served in N C line; drew pension in Marion Co.

Alexander, Dan; 1832 list age 76; served in N C mil; drew pension in Hardeman Co.

Alexander, Elijah; 1832 list age 74; also 1840 Census; served in N C line; drew pension in 1832 in Maury Co; drew pension in 1840 in Marshall Co.

Alexander, Mathew; 1832 list age 77; also 1840 Census; served in N C line; drew pension in Maury Co.

Alexander, William; 1832 list age 71; served in N C line; drew pension in Maury Co.

Alexander, William; 1832 list age 83; served in Va line; drew pension in Knox Co.

Alford, John; 1832 list age 74; served in Va line; drew pension in Davidson Co.

Algood, John; 1832 list age 74; also 1840 Census; served in Va line; drew pension in Monroe Co.

Allen, Charles; 1832 list age 76; also in 1840 Census; served in N C line; drew pension in Williamson Co.

Allen, James; 1840 Census age 81; drew pension in Roane Co.

Allen, John; 1818 list age 75; served in Va troops; drew pension in Madison Co; transferred from Ala; d Aug 10 1824.

Allen, Moses; 1832 list age 80; also 1840 Census; served in Va line; drew pension in Wilson Co.

Allen, Richard; 1832 list age 79; served in Va line; drew pension in Roane Co.

Allen, William; 1828 list; served in Tenn mil; drew pension in Sumner Co; (1812).

Alley, Isaiah; 1840 Census age 91; drew pension in Davidson Co; lived with Thomas Alley.

Alley, James; 1832 list age 81; served in Va line; drew pension in Roane Co.

Alley, Samuel; 1832 list age 87; served in Va line; drew pension in Roane Co.

Allison, John; 1832 list age 71; served in N C line; drew pension in White Co.

Almond, Thomas; 1828 list; served in Lee's Legion; drew pension in Stewart Co.

Almony, John; 1840 Census age 58; drew pension in Sullivan Co; (1812).

Alverson, Elijah; 1832 list age 70; also in 1840 Census; served in Va line; drew pension in White Co.

Amour, Francis; drew pension in Knoxville Agency.

Anderson, Alexander; 1832 list age 72; also in 1840 Census; served in Va mil; drew pension in Stewart Co; lived with John Brown.

Anderson, Alexander; 1840 Census age 85; drew pension in Humphreys Co; lived with Alexander Brown.

Anderson, George; 1832 list age 80; served in N C line; drew pension in Henderson Co.

Anderson, James, Sen; 1832 list age 74; also 1840 Census; served in N C mil; drew pension in Jefferson Co.

Anderson, James; 1832 list age 69; served in Va mil; drew pension in Bedford Co.

Anderson, John; 1832 list age 76; served in Va line; drew pension in Davidson Co.

Anderson, Peter; 1832 list age 79; served in Va mil; drew pension in Hawkins Co.

Anderson, Robert; 1832 list age 73; served in Pa line; drew pension in Jackson Co.

Andrews, Athelstane; 1832 list age 73; served in Mass line; drew pension in Henderson Co.

Andrews, John; 1840 Census age 52; served in 8th reg't inf; drew pension in Henderson Co; (1812).

Andrews, John; 1832 list age 69; served in Va line; drew pension in Williamson Co.

Archer, Isaac, 1818 list age 81; served in Va line; drew pension in Sullivan Co; d Dec 17 1825.

Armstrong, Isaac; 1832 list age 72; served in Va line; drew pension in Anderson Co.

Armstrong, James; 1832 list age 70; served in S C mil; drew pension in Maury Co.

Armstrong, John; 1818 list age 81; served in N C troops; drew pension in Smith Co.

Armstrong, Thomas; 1832 list age 78; also 1840 Census; served in N C line; drew pension in Lincoln Co.

Arnold, Benjamin; 1832 list age 71; served in S C line; drew pension in Warren Co.

Arnold, Francis; 1818 list age 64; served in Va troops; drew pension in White Co.

Ashlock, James; 1818 list age 64; served in Va troops; drew pension in Sumner Co; d Apr 4 1821.

Ashlock, Jesse; 1832 list age 74; also 1840 Census; served in N C mil; drew pension in Overton Co.

Askins, George; 1818 list age 80; served in N C troops drew pension in Rutherford Co.

Aslin, Thomas, 1818 list age 77; served in Va troops; drew pension in Lincoln Co.

Aspley, John; 1818 list age 78; served in N C line; drew pension in Sumner Co.

Atchley, Thomas A; 1832 list age 79; served in N J line; drew pension in Sevier Co; his widow Lydia Atchley 1840 Census age 75 lived with Noah Atchley.

Atkins, Lewis; 1832 list age 77; served in N C line; drew pension in Henry Co.

Atkinson, John; 1832 list age 89; served in Pa mil; drew pension in Williamson Co.

Ausborne, Robert; 1832 list age 80; served in Va troops; drew pension in Sumner Co; d June 10 1833.

Austin, John; 1818 list age 80; served in Va troops; drew pension in Sumner Co; d June 10 1833.

Austin, Stephen; 1840 Census age 82; drew pension in Hardin Co; lived with Saunders Austin.

Avery, George; 1818 list age 70; also 1840 Census; served in N C line; drew pension in Wilson Co.

Awalt, Michael; 1832 list age 77; served in N C line; drew pension in Franklin Co.

Ayers, Henry; 1832 list age 80; served in Va mil; drew pension in Robertson Co; d Sept 22 1833.

Bacchus, William; 1832 list age 78; served in N C line; drew pension in Wilson Co.

Baggel, James; 1818 list age 78; served in S C troops; drew pension in Montgomery Co.

Bailey, John; county of residence unknown; served in 1st reg't inf.; d in service July 4 1814; heirs were: Tabitha, Mary, Thompson B, Hiram and Elizabeth Bailey; (1812).

Baker, Henry B; 1818 list age 77; served in S C line; drew pension in Sevier Co.

Baker, John; 1818 list age 78; served in Ga line; drew pension in Davidson Co.

Baker, Peter; 1818 list age 78; served in N C line; drew pension in White Co; d Feb. 7 1833.

Baker, Samuel; 1818 list age 80; also 1840 Census; served in N C line; drew pension in Giles Co; in 1840 he lived with Robert Chapman.

Baker, Squire; 1818 list age 81; served in Mass troops; drew pension in Stewart Co.

Balch, Amos; 1832 list age 75; served in N C line; drew pension in Bedford Co.

Balis, Elijah; see Bayliss, Elijah.

Ball, Amos; drew pension in Knoxville Agency.

Ballard, Alexander; 1832 list age 82; served in N J line; drew pension in Hawkins Co.

Ballew, Joseph; 1932 list age 77; served in N C line; drew pension in Shelby Co.

Bandy, Epperson; 1828 list; served in Tenn mil; drew pension in Wilson Co; (1812).

Bandy, Thomas 1832 list age 86; served in Va mil; drew pension in Sumner Co.

Banks (alias Brus), Edward; 1818 list age 83; served in Va line; drew pension in Washington Co.

Barclay, John; 1832 list age 72; also 1840 Census; served in N C line; drew pension in Rutherford Co.

Barfield, James; 1828 list; 1840 Census age 58; served in Tenn mil; drew pension in 1828 in Carroll Co; drew pension in 1840 in Lauderdale Co. (1812).

Barefield, James; see Barfield, James.

Barker, George; 1832 list age 75; also 1840 Census; served in N C line drew pension in Maury Co.

Barkett, Frederick; 1832 list age 83; served in Va mil; drew pension in Hawkins Co.

Barkley, James; 1832 list age 73; served in N C mil; drew pension in Warren Co.

Barlow, Henson; 1828 list; served in 7th reg't inf; drew pension in Jefferson Co; d Sept 3 1828; (1812).

Barnard, Carter; see Barnett, Carter.

Barnard, Jonathan; 1818 list age 75; served in N C line; drew pension in Claiborne Co.

Barnes, James; 1832 list age 74; also in 1840 Census; served in Va line; drew pension in Davidson Co.

Barnes, James; 1818 list age 80; served in Va troops; drew pension in Smith Co; d April 1825.

Barnes, John; 1832 list age 74; served in N C mil; drew pension in Sumner Co.

Barnes, William; 1832 list age 82; served in Pa line; drew pension in Sullivan Co.

Barnett, Carter; 1832 list age 71; also 1840 Census; served in N C marines; drew pension in Roane Co; Barnard in 1840 Census.

Barnett, Lance James; 1818 list age 82; served in S C line; drew pension in Franklin Co.

Barnett, Michael; 1832 list age 74; also 1840 Census served in Va mil; drew pension in Jefferson Co.

Barnett, William; 1832 list age 73; also 1840 Census; served in N C line; drew pension in McMinn Co; in 1840 he lived with James Barnett.

Barns, William; 1840 Census age 75; drew pension in McNairy Co.

Barr, James; 1828 list; served in Tenn Rangers; drew pension in Sumner Co; (1812).

Barron, William; 1832 list age 74; served in N C line; drew pension in Washington Co.

Bartlett, John; 1818 list age 70; served in Va line; drew pension in Davidson Co; transferred from Jefferson Co Ky.

Bashaw, Peter; 1832 list age 71; also 1840 Census; served in Va mil; drew pension in Davidson Co.

Bass, James; 1832 list age 74; also in 1840 Census; served in Va mil; drew pension in 1832 in Bedford Co; drew pension in 1840 in Marshall Co.

Basset, Nathaniel; 1832 list age 76; served in Va mil; drew pension in Hawkins Co.

Bassford, James; 1828 list; served in 39th U S inf; drew pension in Madison Co; (1812).

Baswell, David; 1832 list age 74; served in Va line; drew pension in Williamson Co.

Bates, Isaac, 1828 list; served in Col. Armstrong's reg't; drew pension in Shelby Co; (1812).

Bates, Jacob; 1832 list age 73; served in N C mil; drew pension in Sullivan Co.

Bay, Andrew; 1832 list age 78; served in N C line; drew pension in Wilson Co.

Bayless, John; 1818 list age 84; served in Va line; drew pension in Knox Co.

Bayliss, Elijah; 1832 list age 74; also 1840 Census; served in Va line; drew pension in Sumner Co.

Beacham, John W; 1840 Census age 33; drew pension in Wilson Co; too young for Revolution or 1812.

Bealer, Jacob; 1832 list age 72; served in Va line; drew pension in Sullivan Co.

Beard, Robert; 1832 list age 71; served in Va line; drew pension in Washington Co; d Aug. 6 1833.

Beard, Samuel; 1832 list age 80; served in Va line; drew pension in Williamson Co.

Beard, William; 1832 list age 72; also 1840 Census; served in Pa line; drew pension in Sumner Co; in 1840 he lived with Frank Yourn.

Bearden, John; 1832 list age 89; served in S C line; drew pension in Bedford Co.

Beasley, Isom; 1840 Census age 87; drew pension in Smith Co.

Beaty, Andrew; 1832 list age 74; served in N C line; drew pension in Fentress Co.

Beaty, James; 1832 list age 79; served in N C line; drew pension in Rutherford Co.

Beaty, Walter; 1818 list age 62; served in Va line; drew pension in Hawkins Co; his widow, Mary Beaty, 1840 Census age 81; lived with Samuel Beatty.

Beavert, John; 1818 list age 75; served in N C line; drew pension in Rutherford Co.

Beggs, John; drew pension in Jonesboro Agency.

Belcher, Bartlett; 1832 list age 69; also 1840 Census; served in Va line; drew pension in Hawkins Co.

Bell, James; 1840 Census age 79; drew pension in Hawkins Co.

Bell, Lieut. John; 1828 list; served in Russell's Spies; drew pension in Madison Co; (1812).

Bell, Thomas; 1832 list age 78; served in Va line; drew pension in Washington Co.

Bell, Thomas; 1832 list age 73; served in N C line; drew pension in Montgomery Co.

Bell, William; 1832 list age 86; also 1840 Census; served in N C line; drew pension in Montgomery Co.

Belloat, James; 1840 Census age 80; drew pension in Fayette Co where he lived with C S Belloat.

Bender, Daniel; 1832 list age 84; served in N C line; drew pension in Sumner Co.

Bennett, Joseph; 1840 Census age 83; drew pension in Rutherford Co where he lived with Thomas Bennett.

Benson, Levi; 1832 list age 83; served in Del line; drew pension in Lincoln Co.

Benson, Spencer; 1832 list age 78; also 1840 Census; served in Del line; drew pension in 1832 in Rhea Co; drew pension in 1840 in Mc-Minn Co where he lived with John Benson.

Bentley, Jeremiah; 1818 list age 75; also 1840 Census served in Va line; drew pension in 1832 in Giles Co; drew pension in 1840 in Lawrence Co.

Benton, David; 1818 list age 77; served in N C line; drew pension in Warren Co.

Berk, Elihu; 1840 Census age 75; drew pension in Franklin Co where he lived with Alexander Donelson.

Berry, Enoch; 1832 list age 71; also in 1840 Census; served in N C line; drew pension in 1832 in Warren Co; drew pension in 1840 in Cannon Co.

Berry, John; 1828 list; served in Penn mil; drew pension in Monroe Co, transferred from Penn.

Berry, Sanford; 1832 list age 71; served in S C line; drew pension in Franklin Co.

Berryhill, Alexander; 1832 list age 71; served in N C line; drew pension in Franklin Co.

Bertram, William; 1840 Census age 81; drew pension in White Co.

Bethel, John; 1840 Census age 84; drew pension in Grainger Co.

Bevert, John; 1840 Census age 86; drew pension in DeKalb Co.

Bibee, Thomas; 1832 list age 100; served in Va line; drew pension in Cocke Co.

Biffle, Jacob; 1832 list age 71; also 1840 Census; served in S C line; drew pension in Maury Co.

Billington, Ezekial; 1832 list age 75; also 1840 Census; served in N J line; drew pension in 1832 in Bedford Co; drew pension in 1840 in Marshall Co.

Bingham, Benjamin; 1832 list age 78; served in Va mil; drew pension in Blount Co.

Bingham, William; 1832 list age 77; also 1840 Census; served in N C mil; drew pension in 1832 in Bedford Co; drew pension in 1840 'n Marshall Co.

Binkley, Lieut. Adam; 1832 list age 94; served in N C line; drew pension in Davidson Co.

Birdsong, John; 1832 list age 77; also 1840 Census; drew pension in Fayette Co.

Birdwell, Benjamin; 1832 list age 69; also 1840 Census; served in N C line; drew pension in Sullivan Co.

Blackburn, James; 1818 list age 74; served in Va line; drew pension in Anderson Co.

Blackmore, George; 1832 list age 72; served in S C line; drew pension in Lincoln Co.

Blackmore, George D; 1832 list age 74; served in Md line; drew pension in Lincoln Co.

Blackwell, David; 1832 list age 75; also 1840 Census; served in Va mil; drew pension in Roane Co.

Blair, Lieut. John; 1828 list; drew pension in Washington Co; d July 13 1818; (1812).

Blair, Samuel; 1832 list age 76; served in N C line; drew pension in McMinn Co.

Blair, Thomas; 1832 list age 70; served in S C line; drew pension in Maury Co.

Blalock, Charles; 1818 list age 81; also 1840 list; served in N C line; drew pension in Wilson Co.

Blalock, Daniel; 1832 list age 83; also 1840 Census; served in N C line; drew pension in Fayette Co; in 1840 he lived with Margaret Hurley.

Blalock, Lieut John; 1832 list age 72; served in Va line; drew pension in Carter Co.

Blanton, Thomas; 1818 list age 74; also 1840 Census; served in Va troops; drew pension in Rutherford Co.

Bledsoe, Jacob; 1832 list age 72; also 1840 Census; served in N C troops; drew pension in Bedford Co.

Bletcher, Jacob; 1818 list age 74; served in N C line; drew pension in Bedford Co.

Blevins, Daniel; 1818 list age 81; served in N C mil; drew pension in Morgan Co.

Blevins, Henry; 1832 list age 75; also 1840 Census; served in N C line; drew pension in Hawkins Co.

Blurton, Edward; 1818 list age 76; served in N C troops; drew pension in Wilson Co.

Bobh, Seth, Sen; 1832 list age 74; served in Va line; drew pension in Greene Co.

Bogle, Margaret, widow; drew pension in 1845 in Blount Co.

Boin, William; 1832 list age 78; served in Va line; drew pension in Hawkins Co.

Boisseau, John; 1832 list age 69; served in Va line; drew pension in Simpson Co according to 1832 list; (there is no Simpson Co in Tenn.)

Bolen, John; 1832 list age 74; served in Va line; drew pension in Sullivan Co.

Bolen, William; 1840 Census age 83; drew pension in Sullivan Co.

Bolin, James; 1832 list age 85; served in Pa line; drew pension in Rutherford Co.

Bolling, Edmund; 1818 list age 74; served in Va line; drew pension in Greene Co.

Bonar, Henry; 1832 list age 79; served in Pa line; drew pension in Davidson Co.

Bond, William; 1832 list age 79; also 1840 Census; served in N C line; drew pension in Hawkins Co.

Bonner, John; 1832 list age 78; served in N J mil; drew pension in Wilson Co.

Bonner, William; 1832 list age 78; served in N C mil; drew pension in Henry Co.

Boon, Susanna, widow; 1840 Census age 79; drew pension in Smith Co.

Booth, George C; 1832 list age 76; also 1840 Census; served in Va line; drew pension in Rutherford Co.

Bose, Samuel; drew pension in Knoxville Agency.

Boston, Christopher; 1832 list age 74; also 1840 Census; served in N C mil; drew pension in 1832 in Claiborne Co; drew pension in 1840 in Monroe Co.

Bottom, Miles; 1832 list age 82; served in N C mil; drew pension in Warren Co.

Bowden, Elias; 1832 list age 72; also 1840 Census; served in Va line; drew pension in Henry Co.

Bowden, William; 1832 list age 92; served in N C line; drew pension in Maury Co.

Bowen, Charles; served in Rev; drew pension in Knoxville Agency; transferred to Ind 1833.

Bowers, James; 1832 list age 75; also 1840 Census; served in N J line; drew pension in Maury Co.

Bowers, Leonard; 1832 list age 74; also 1840 Census; served in Va line; drew pension in Carter Co.

Bowman, Daniel; 1840 Census age 82; drew pension in Rutherford Co.

Bowman, John; 1818 list age 81; also 1840 Census; served in Va line; drew pension in Roane Co.

Bowman, Samuel; 1832 list age 75; served in Va line; drew pension in Rutherford Co.

Bowman, Sparling; 1832 list age 82; served in Md line; drew pension in Greene Co.

Bowman, William; 1832 list age 76; served in Va mil; drew pension in Knox Co.

Box, Edward; 1832 list age 78; served in S C mil; drew pension in Perry Co.

Box, Samuel; 1832 list age 89; served in S C mil; drew pension in Jefferson Co.

Boy, Jacob; 1832 list age 83; served in Va mil; drew pension in Sullivan Co; d May 20 1833.

Boyd, John; 1818 list age 73; also 1840 Census; served in Pa line; drew pension in Blount Co.

Boyd, William; 1832 list age 73; also 1840 Census; served in N C line; drew pension in Roane Co.

Boydston, William; 1832 list age 81; served in Va mil; drew pension in Cocke Co.

Boyers, Michael; 1832 list age 75; served in Pa line; drew pension in Claiborne Co.

Bradberry, John; 1840 Census age 104; drew pension in Giles Co; he lived with J. Bradberry.

Braden, John; 1832 list age 74; also 1840 Census; served in Va line; drew pension in Claiborne Co.

Bradford, William; 1818 list age 74; served in Va troops; drew pension in Sumner Co.

Bradley, John; 1832 list age 82; served in Va line; drew pension in Rutherford Co.

Bradley, John; 1832 list age 77; also 1840 Census; served in Va mil; drew pension in Rutherford Co.

Bradley, Richard; 1818 list; served in N C troops; drew pension in Sumner Co; d Aug 20 1821.

Bradshaw, Benjamin; 1840 Census age 82; drew pension in Jefferson Co.

Bragg, William; 1832 list age 69; also 1840 Census; served in Va mil; drew pension in Cocke Co.

Brakebill, Peter; 1832 list age 74; served in Va line; drew pension in Monroe Co.

Brandon, Charles; 1832 list age 85; served in Va mil; drew pension in Bedford Co.

Brandon, Josiah; 1832 list age 74; also 1840 Census; drew pension in Lincoln Co.

Brannon, Thomas; 1818 list age 100; served in N C line; drew pension in Bledsoe Co.

Brashears, Morris; 1832 list age 78; served in Md line; drew pension in Roane Co.

Bratcher, Charles; 1832 list age 72; served in Va line; drew pension in Campbell Co; d Aug 11 1833.

Bratcher William; 1818 list age 94; served in S C troops; drew pension in Maury Co.

Brawley, William; 1832 list age 71; served in N C line; drew pension in Maury Co.

Brechen, William Sr; 1832 list age 79; served in N C line; drew pension in Bedford Co.

Breeden, Charles; 1832 list age 81; served in N C line; drew pension in Wilson Co.

Breeden, Enoch; 1840 Census age 82; drew pension in Franklin Co.

Bregins, John; 1840 Census age 67; drew pension in Perry Co; (1812).

Brent, John; 1818 list age 81; served in Va troops; drew pension in Smith Co; d Jul 20 1833.

Brevard, Benjamin; 1832 list age 72; served in N C line; drew pension in Humphreys Co.

Brewer, William; 1832 list age 82; served in N C line; drew pension in Blount Co.

Brigger, Robert; 1832 list age 73; served in N C line; drew pension in Montgomery Co.

Briggs, John; 1832 list age 82; served in Pa line; drew pension in Greene Co.

Bright, James; 1818 list age 82; served in Md line; drew pension in Sullivan Co.

Brimer, William; 1832 list age 75; served in N C mil; drew pension in Sevier Co; d Apr 12 1834.

Brinkley, Adam; 1832 list age 94; served in N C line; drew pension in Davidson Co.

Britt, Obed; 1832 list age 75; served in Va mil; drew pension in Perry Co.

Brittain, Philip; 1818 list age 74; served in N C line; drew pension in Bedford Co; transferred from Orange Co N C

Britton, Lieut Joseph; 1818 list age 65; also 1840 Census; served in Va line; drew pension in Hawkins Co.

Brizendine, Leroy; 1832 list age 73; served in Va line; drew pension in Sumner Co.

Broadway, John; 1818 list age 74; also 1840 Census; served in S C troops; drew pension in Wayne Co.

Brochus, John; 1818 list age 77; served in Va line; drew pension in Grainger Co.

Broiles, Daniel; see Broyles.

Brook, Dudley; 1832 list age 72; served in Va line; drew pension in Robertson Co.

Brooks, David; 1832 list age 75; served in Va line; drew pension in Claiborne Co.

Brooks, John; 1832 list age 82; served in Md line; drew pension in Fayette Co.

Brooks, Joseph; 1828 list; 2nd reg't U S Rifles; drew pension in Overton Co; (1812).

Brooks, Littleton; 1832 list age 76; also 1840 Census; served in N C line; drew pension in Hawkins Co.

Brooks, Thomas; 1832 list age 74; served in Va line; drew pension in Hawkins Co.

Brotherton, William; 1818 list age 75; served in N C line; drew pension in Greene Co.

Brown, Aaron; 1832 list age 78; served in Va line; drew pension in Monroe Co.

Brown, Arthur; 1818 list age 72; also 1840 Census; served in N C line; drew pension in Carroll Co; transferred from Caldwell Co Ky.

Brown, Benjamin; 1832 list age 76; also 1840 Census; served in N C troops; drew pension in McMinn Co.

Brown, Benjamin; 1832 list age 83; served in N C line; drew pension in White Co.

Brown, David E; 1818 list age 84; served in N C line; drew pension in Davidson Co.

Brown, George; 1832 list age 74; served in N C line; drew pension in Washington Co.

Brown, Hiram; served in 1st reg't Rifles; drew pension in Sullivan Co; died in service Nov or Dec 1813; his heir was Polly Ann Brown; (1812).

Brown, Hubbard; drew pension in Jackson Agency.

Brown, Isham; 1818 list age 85; served in Va line; drew pension in Giles Co.

Brown, Isaiah; 1832 list age 74;. served in N C line; drew pension in Roane Co; d Apr 29 1833.

Brown, Jacob; 1832 list age 82; also 1840 Census; served in N C line; drew pension in Washington Co.

Brown, Jacob; 1832 list age 73; served in S C mil; drew pension in Washington Co.

Brown, Jacob; 1832 list age 73; served in S C mil; drew pension in Washington Co.

Brown, James; 1832 list age 75; served in Va line; drew pension in Davidson Co.

Brown, James; 1818 list age 80; served in Va troops; drew pension in Smith Co; d June 21 1832.

Brown, Jeremiah; 1840 Census age 85; drew pension in Jackson Co.

Brown, John; 1840 Census age 80; drew pension in Rutherford Co.

Brown, Joseph; 1832 list age 75; also 1840 Census; served in Pa mil; drew pension in Knox Co.

Brown, Lieut. Morgan; 1832 list age 77; served in S C line; drew pension in Davidson Co.

Brown, Moses; 1832 list age 82; served in S C line; drew pension in Davidson Co.

Brown, Robert 1832 list age 76; also 1840 Census; served in N C line; drew pension in Warren Co.

Brown, Richard; 1832 list age 78; served in S C line; drew pension in Giles Co.

Brown, Stephen; 1832 list age 78; served in Va mil; drew pension in Bledsoe Co.

Brown, Thomas; 1832 list age 81; also 1840 Census; served in N C line; drew pension Warren Co.

Brown, Thomas; 1832 list age 71; also 1840 Census; served in Va line; drew pension in Grainger Co.

Brown, William; 1840 Census age 70; drew pension in Lincoln Co; lived with Joshua B Brown.

Brown, William; 1832 list age 82; served in N J mil; drew pension in Bedford Co.

Broyles, 1832 list age 73; served in Va line; drew pension in McMinn Co.

Broyles, Daniel; 1832 list age 73; also 1840 Census; served in Va line; drew pension in 1832 in McMinn Co; drew pension in 1840 in Rhea Co; lived with Cornelius Broyles.

Broyles, Michael; 1832 list age 94; served in Va line; drew pension in Washington Co.

Bruce, George; 1818 list age 73; also 1840 Census; served in N C troops; drew pension in Rutherford Co; lived with Joseph Arthur.

Bruce, John; 1840 Census age 45; drew pension in Rutherford Co; (1812).

Bruce, William; 1832 list age 72; also 1840 Census; served in Va line; drew pension in Rutherford Co.

Brummett, Thomas; 1818 list age 79; also 1840 Census; served in Va Continental line; drew pension in Anderson Co.

Bruner, Jacob; 1832 list age 71; also 1840 Census; served in Md line; drew pension in Greene Co where he lived with Ide Bruner.

Brus (alias Banks) Edward; 1818 list age 83; served in Va line; drew pension in Washington Co.

Bryan, Michael; 1818 list age 71; served in Va troops; drew pension in Rutherford Co.

Bryant, James; 1832 list age 85; served in Va line; drew pension in Grainger Co.

Bryant, Jesse; 1818 list; served in Va line; drew pension in Cocke Co.

Bryant, Robert; 1840 Census age 93; drew pension in Blount Co; lived with Thomas Bryant.

Bryant, Thomas; 1832 list age 75; also 1840 Census; served in Va line; drew pension in Greene Co; lived with Austin Bryant.

Bryant, William; 1818 list age 99; served in Va line; drew pension in Davidson Co.

Bryson, Samuel; 1832 list age 80; served in N C line; drew pension in Wilson Co.

Buck, Ephraim; 1840 Census age 49; drew pension in Carter Co; (1812).

Buckley, James; 1832 list age 72; served in Va line; drew pension in Weakley Co.

Bullard, John; 1832 list age 79; served in Va line; drew pension in Rutherford Co.

Buntin, William; 1840 Census age 73; drew pension in Henry Co.

Burford, Philip T; 1832 list age 72; served in N C line; drew pension in Fayette Co.

Burk, Robert; 1832 list age 70; served in N C line; drew pension in Roane Co.

Burke (see Berk), Elihu; 1840 Census; drew pension in Franklin Co.

Burke, Elisha; 1818 list age 71; served in N C line; drew pension in Marion Co.

Burke, Isom; 1832 list 73; served in Ga line; drew pension in McNairy Co.

Burke, Joseph; 1832 list age 72; also 1840 Census; served in N C mil; drew pension in Cocke Co.

Burkes, Samuel; 1832 list age 69; served in N C line; drew pension in Rutherford Co.

Burkett, Frederick; 1832 list age 82; served in Va line; drew pension in Greene Co.

Burnett, William; 1840 Census age 91; drew pension in Rutherford Co.

Burns, John; 1832 list age 81; served in N C line; drew pension in Bedford Co.

Burns, John; 1828 list; served in Tenn mil; drew pension in Hardeman Co; (1812).

Burns, Jacob; 1832 list age 77; served in Va line; drew pension in Smith Co; d Oct 1 1832.

Burns, Laird; 1832 list age 78; also 1840 Census; served in S C line; drew pension in Roane Co.

Burritt, William; 1832 list age 75; served in Va line; drew pension in Rutherford Co.

Burton, Henry; 1818 list age 75; served in N C troops; drew pension in Humphreys Co.

Busby, Isham; 1832 list age 75; served in N C line; drew pension in Smith Co.

Bush, Enoch; 1832 list age 86; served in Va line; drew pension in Roane Co.

Bushong, George; 1840 Census age 48; served in Tenn mil; drew pension in Sullivan Co; (1812).

Bussell (Bussle) Mathew; 1832 list; also 1840 Census age 93; served in Va line; drew pension in Claiborne Co.

Bussell, William; 1832 list age 75; also 1840 Census; served in N C line; drew pension in Hawkins Co.

Butler, Benjamin; 1832 list age 69; served in Va line; drew pension in Henderson Co.

Butler, Thomas; 1832 list age 70; served in N C mil; drew pension in Morgan Co.

Butler, William; 1832 list age 72; served in N C line; drew pension in Anderson Co.

Butler, William; 1828 list; served in Tenn mil; drew pension in Jackson Co; (1812).

Butler, Zachariah; 1832 list age 80; served in Md mil; drew pension in Sullivan Co.

Butler, Zachariah; 1832 list age 70; also 1840 Census; served in Va line; drew pension in Maury Co.

Byerly, Michael; 1832 list age 77; served in Va line; drew pension in Washington Co.

Byers, William; 1832 list age 87; served in S C line; drew pension in Williamson Co.

Byles, Charles; 1832 list age 85; served in N C line; drew pension in Henry Co.

Bynum, John; 1832 list age 77: served in Ga line; drew pension in Rutherford Co.

Bynum, John; 1840 Census age 83; drew pension in Cannon Co. (probably same as above).

Byron, Henry; drew pension in Jonesboro Agency.

Cabbage, Adam; 1840 Census age 85; drew pension in Grainger Co.

Cabbage, John; 1832 list age 76; also 1840 Census; served in Va mil; drew pension in Campbell County; lived with Champion Waters.

Cabler, Frederick; 1832 list age 76; also 1840 Census; served in N C line; drew pension in Davidson Co; lived with John Corbett.

Cain, William; 1818 list age 87; served in Va troops; drew pension in Rutherford County; d Oct 22 1828.

Caldwell, George; 1832 list age 73; served in Va line; drew pension in Blount County.

Caldwell, Jeb; 1828 list; served in Tripplett's reg't; drew pension in Knox Co; transferred from Va; d Feb 25 1829; his pension dated from 1785; (Rev and 1812).

Caldwell, William, Sen; 1832 list age 71; also 1840 Census; served in N C line; drew pension in Jefferson Co.

Callahan; 1832 list age 78; served in N C line; drew pension in Giles County.

Calvert, Willis; his widow, Rebecca, lived in Kenton Co Ky where she drew pension in 1835 age 47; he d in Nashville Tenn June 15 1849; (1812).

Calwell, William; 1832 list age 77; also 1840 Census; served in S C line; drew pension in Franklin Co; lived with William Cowan.

Campbell, David; 1832 list age 73; served in Va line; drew pension in McNairy Co.

Campbell, James; 1832 list age 75; also 1840 Census; served in N C line.

Campbell, James; 1832 list age 77; also 1840 Census; served in Va line; drew pension in Carter Co; lived with James Filyour, Jr.

Campbell, Jeremiah; 1832 list age 72; also 1840 Census; served in N C line; drew pension in Carter Co.

Campbell, John; 1832 list age 69; served in Va line; drew pension in Cocke Co.

Campbell, Joseph; 1832 list age 72; also 1840 Census; served in Va line; drew pension in Hamilton Co.

Campbell, Richard; 1840 Census age 82; drew pension in Hickman Co.

Campbell, Lieut Robert; 1832 list age 75; also 1840 Census; served in Va line; drew pension in Hawkins Co.

Campbell, Solomon; 1818 list age 79; served in N C line; drew pension in Bedford Co.

Cannon, Pugh; 1832 list age 78; also 1840 Census; served in N C line; drew pension in McNairy Co; lived with Terrill Siveat.

Cannon, William; drew pension in Jonesboro Agency.

Cantwell, John; 1832 list age 89; served in S C line; drew pension in Hawkins Co.

Capeshaw, Catherine; widow, filed claim in Blount Co aft 1840.

Cardwell, Perrin; 1832 list age 70; also 1840 Census; served in Va line; drew pension in Knox Co.

Carlisle, William; 1832 list age 68; also 1840 Census; drew pension in Jackson Co; lived with William Morse.

Carmack, Cornelius; 1832 list age 75; also 1840 Census; served in Va line; drew pension in Overton Co; lived with John Carmack.

Carmichael, John 1832 list age 77; served in Pa line; drew pension in Cocke Co.

Carnahan, Andrew; 1832 list age 72; served in N C line; drew pension in Rutherford Co.

Carnes, Philip; 1832 list age 73; served in N C line; drew pension in McNairy Co.

Carney, John, Sen.; 1818 list age 86; also 1840 Census age 106; served in N C troops; drew pension in 1818 in Smith Co; drew pension in 1840 in Sumner Co.

Carr, Gideon; 1832 list age 83; also 1840 Census; served in Va line; drew pension in Dickson Co; lived with John Carr.

Carr, James; 1832 list age 76; served in Va line; drew pension in Giles Co.

Carr, John F; 1832 list age 69; served in Va mil; drew pension in Maury Co.

Carr, William; 1828 list; county of residence unknown; (1812).

Carr, William, 2nd; 1818 list age 73; served in Va line; drew pension in Knox Co; d Nov 5 1824;

Carr, William; 1818 list age 72; served in Conn line; drew pension in Knox Co.

Carr, William; 1832 list age 79; served in N C mil; drew pension in Sullivan Co.

Carroll, Daniel; 1832 list age 69; served in Va line; drew pension in Wayne Co.

Carroll, David; 1840 Census age 77; drew pension in Cannon Co; lived with George W. Thurston.

Carroll, David; 1818 list age 84; served in S C line; drew pension in Lincoln Co; transferred from Lauderdale Co Ala.

Carroll, William; 1832 list age 79; served in N C line; drew pension in Roane Co.

Carson, Henry; 1832 list age 79; served in S C line; drew pension in Weakley Co.

Carson, Robert; 1832 list; also 1840 Census age 87; served in Va mil; drew pension in Warren Co; lived with Andrew Michael.

Carson, Thomas (alias John Perkins); 1832 list age 69; served in Va mil; drew pension in Franklin Co.

Carswell, John; 1832 list age 70; served in Va line; drew pension in Overton Co.

Carter, Charles; 1832 list age 74; served in Va line; drew pension in Smith Co.

Carter, Charles; 1832 list age 71; also 1840 Census; served in N C line; drew pension in McMinn Co.

Carter, Daniel; 1832 list age 73; served in S C line; drew pension in Maury Co.

Carter, Elizabeth, widow of Landon Carter; 1840 Census age 75; drew pension in Carter Co; she lived with Benjamin Brewer.

Carter, John, Sen; 1832 list age 78; also 1840 Census; served in N C line; drew pension in Greene Co; in 1840 he lived with Ezekiel Carter.

Carter, Samuel, Sen; 1832 list age 80; also 1840 Census; served in Va line; drew pension in 1832 in Monroe Co; drew pension in 1840 in Polk Co; lived with Amos Carter.

Carter, Thomas; 1818 list age 75; served in Va line; drew pension in Knox Co; d Jul 25 1825.

Caruthers, James; 1832 list age 74; also 1840 Census; served in Va line; drew pension in Blount Co.

Caruthers, Robert; 1832 list age 84; served in N C line; drew pension in Bedford Co.

Casey, John; 1832 list age 71; also 1840 Census; served in Va line; drew pension in Davidson Co; lived with Charles S Casey.

Cashin, David; 1832 list age 75; served in Va mil; drew pension in Weakley Co.

Cason, James; see Cayson.

Cathcart, Joseph; 1832 list age 87; served in S C line; drew pension in Monroe Co.

Caulk, Jacob; 1818 list; served in Del troops; drew pension in Rutherford Co.

Cauly, Francis (see Coley, Francis); 1840 Census age 100; drew pension in Smith Co.

Cayson, James; 1832 list age 76; also 1840 Census; served in Va line; drew pension in Jackson Co; lived with Edmund Cason.

Chambers, John 1832 list age 81; also 1840 Census; served in Va line; drew pension in Carroll Co; in 1840 he lived with Wilson Chambers.

Chandley, William; 1818 list age 79; served in Va line; drew pension in Greene Co; d Sept. 22, 1827.

Chapman, Benjamin 1832 list age 74; also 1840 Census; served in Md line; drew pension in Roane Co.

Chapman, John H; 1832 list age 68; served in Va line; drew pension in Anderson Co.

Chapman, Lucy, widow; 1840 Census age 70; drew pension in Fentress Co.

Chapman, Robert; 1818 list age 74; served in S C line; drew pension in Sevier Co.

Charlton, Jacob; 1832 list age 92; served in Va line; drew pension in Hawkins Co.

Charlton, John; 1832 list age 73; served in Va mil; drew pension in Davidson Co.

Cherry, Joshua; 1832 list age 72; served in N C line; drew pension in Bedford Co.

Cheatham, Benjamin; 1832 list age 83; also 1840 Census; served in Va line; drew pension in Giles Co.

Cheek, Richard; 1840 Census age 79; drew pension in Jefferson Co.

Chester, John; 1832 list age 86; also 1840 Census; served in N C line; drew pension in Weakley Co.

Chester, John; 1818 list age 79; also 1840 Census; served in Va line; drew pension in Sullivan Co.

Childress, David; 1818 list age 73; also 1840 Census; served in Ga line; drew pension in Sullivan Co; lived with W P Nelms.

Childress, John; 1832 list age 79; served in N C mil; drew pension in Rutherford Co.

Childress, John; 1832 list age 74; also 1840 Census; served in Va line; drew pension in Knox Co.

Childress, Mitchell; 1832 list age 83; also in 1840 Census; served in N C line; drew pension in Knox Co.

Childress, Thomas; 1832 list age 84; served in Va line; drew pension in Lincoln Co.

Childress, William; 1832 list age 72; served in S C line; drew pension in White Co.

Chiles, Hezekiah; 1832 list age 74; served in N C mil; drew pension in Lincoln Co.

Chilton, George; see George Shelton.

Chitwood, James; 1832 list age 82; served in N C line; drew pension in Campbell Co.

Christian, John; 1818 list age 63; served in N C troops; drew pension in Smith Co.

Choate, Christopher; 1832 list age 84; served in S C line; drew pension in McNairy Co.

Chumley, Daniel; 1832 list age 75; served in Va line; drew pension in Wilson Co.

Chunn, Sylvester; 1818 list; also 1840 Census; served in Va troops; drew pension in Maury Co in 1818; drew pension in Marshall Co in 1840.

Clack, Sterling; 1818 list age 74; served in Va troops; drew pension in Sumner Co.

Clampit, ———, widow of Govey (?) Clampit; filed pension claim in Blount Co in 1844.

Clark, Benjamin; 1832 list age 71; also 1840 Census; served in N C line; drew pension in 1832 in Monroe Co; drew pension in 1840 in Roane Co.

Clark, Burgess; 1832 list age 72; also 1840 Census; served in N C line; drew pension in White Co.

Clark, George; 1832 list age 84; also 1840 Census; served in N C mil; drew pension in Dickson Co; lived with Benjamin Clark.

Clark, Henry; 1828 list; served in Tenn mil; drew pension in Robertson Co; (1812).

Clark, Lieut James, Sen; 1832 list age 75; also 1840 Census; served in N C line; drew pension in Madison Co.

Clark, James; 1832 list age 71; served in Va line; drew pension in Blount Co.

Clark, Lieut John; 1832 list age 76; served in N C mil; drew pension in Washington Co.

Clark, John; 1832 list age 73; also 1840 Census; served in N C line; drew pension in Rutherford Co.

Clark, John; 1818 list age 91; served in Va line; drew pension in Blount Co.

Clark, Robert; 1832 list age 73; served in Va line; drew pension in Tipton Co.

Clay, John; 1832 list age 79; served in Va line; drew pension in Rutherford Co.

Clay, William; 1832 list age 74; also 1840 Census; served in Va line; drew pension in Grainger Co.

Clayborn, John; 1832 list age 74; served in Va line; drew pension in Knox Co.

Clearwaters, Benjamin; 1818 list age 86; served in Va troops; drew pension in Madison Co.

Cleburne, John; 1840 Census age 82; drew pension in Sumner Co where he lived with George Cleburne.

Clemmens, John; 1832 list age 81; served in N C line; drew pension in Jackson Co.

Clemmons, Thomas; 1832 list age 83; served in N C line; drew pension in Wilson Co.

Click, Henry; 1840 Census age 59; served in 4th inf; drew pension in Cocke Co; (1812).

Clopton, Walter; 1832 list age 77; served in Va line; drew pension in Wilson Co.

Cloyd, William; 1832 list age 82; served in Pa line; drew pension in Washington Co.

Coal, Willis; 1832 list age 71; served in N C line; drew pension in Fentress Co.

Coats, William; 1818 list age 73; also 1840 Census; served in Va line; drew pension in Davidson Co; lived with Beverly E Coats.

Coatney, James; 1832 list age 85; served in Va line; drew pension in Greene Co.

Cobb, Ethelred; 1828 list; served in Dark's U S reg't; drew pension in Lincoln Co; (1812).

Cobb, Lieut Pharoah; 1832 list age 82; also 1840 Census; served in N C line; drew pension in Hawkins Co; lived with Jessie Cobb.

Cochrane, Ensign Samuel, Sen; 1832 list age 74; also 1840 Census; served in Va line; drew pension in Sumner Co.

Cochran, William; 1840 Census age 73; drew pension in Benton Co; lived with J T Florence.

Cock, John; 1832 list age 78; served in N C mil; drew pension in Warren Co.

Cocke, William; 1832 list age 73; served in Va line; drew pension in Rutherford Co.

Coffee, Benjamin; 1832 list age 87; served in N C line; drew pension in Hawkins Co; d Jan 4 1834.

Coffee, James; 1832 list age 77; served in Pa line; drew pension in Bedford Co.

Cole, James; 1832 list age 79; served in N C line; drew pension in Carroll Co.

Cole, Stephen; 1832 list age 78; served in S C line; drew pension in Robertson Co.

Cole, Willis; see Coal, Willis.

Coleman, Hardy; 1832 list age 76; served in N C line; drew pension in Sumner Co.

Coleman, John; 1818 list age 81; served in Ga line; drew pension in Stewart Co.

Coleman, Spencer; 1832 list age 82; served in Va line; drew pension in Monroe Co.

Coleman, William; 1832 list age 72; served in N C mil; drew pension in Cocke Co.

Coley, Francis; 1832 list age 78; served in Va line; drew pension in Smith Co; see Francis Cauly.

Coley, James; 1832 list age 76; served in N C line; drew pension in Humphreys Co.

Collins, Lewis; 1840 Census age 87; drew pension in Grainger Co.

Collinsworth, John; served in Rev; drew pension in Grainger Co; transferred to Ill.

Colly (Corley) Austin; 1832 list age 77; also 1840 Census; served in Va line; drew pension in Wison Co.

Colly, William; 1832 list age 82; also 1840 Census; served in Va mil; drew pension in Wilson Co.

Combs, Gilbert; 1832 list age 74; served in N J line; drew pension in McNairy Co.

Compton, Jeremiah H; 1832 list age 70; also 1840 Census; served in Va mil; drew pension in Sevier Co; lived with Cyrus Compton.

Conklin, John; drew pension in Knoxville Agency.

Connelly, John; 1832 list age 74; served in Va mil; drew pension in Bedford Co.

Conner, Isaac; served in 7th reg't inf; drew pension in Knox Co; d in service May 14 1814; his heirs were: Kitty, Nancy, Lucinda, Viney, Ann and Thomas Conner; (1812).

Connor, Maxmillion; 1832 list age 71; served in Va mil; drew pension in Greene Co.

Connor, Thomas; 1832 list age 77; also 1840 Census; served in Pa line; drew pension in Wilson Co.

Conway, James; 1818 list age 91; served in Va line; drew pension in Knox Co; transferred from Greenville S C in Sept 1819.

Conway, Sarah, widow of Henry Conway; drew pension in Jonesboro Agency.

Cook, Alston; 1828 list; drew pension in Maury Co; transferred from N C; (1812).

Cook, Ensign Henry; 1832 list age 74; served in Va line; drew pension in Williamson Co; d June 19 1833.

Cook, Henry; 1832 list age 81; served in N C line; drew pension in Carroll Co.

Cook, John; 1832 list age 74; served in Pa line; drew pension in Sevier Co.

Cooke, John; 1832 list age 78; served in Va line; drew pension in Williamson Co.

Coon, Conrad; 1832 list age 78; served in S C line; drew pension in Robertson Co.

Coon, John C: 1840 Census age 85; drew pension in Robertson Co; he lived with Eliza Saunders.

Coop, Horatio; served in Rev; drew pension in Knoxville Agency.

Coop, Horatio; 1832 list age 76; also 1840 Census; served in Md mil; drew pension in Bedford Co; lived with James Coop.

Cooper, Alexander; 1832 list 1840 Census age 77; served in N C mil; drew pension in White Co.

Cooper, Dabney; 1832 list age 75; also 1840 Census; served in Va line; drew pension in Smith Co.

Cooper, E; 1840 Census age 45; drew pension in McMinn Co.

Cooper, James; 1832 list age 76; served in N C line; drew pension in Hawkins Co.

Cooper, Richard; 1818 list age 77; served in Va line; drew pension in Rhea Co.

Cope, Barakias; 1828 list; served in Tenn mil; drew pension in Blount Co; (1812).

Copeland, Benjamin; 1840 Census age 76; drew pension in Marshall Co.

Copeland, Henry; drew pension in Jonesboro Agency.

Copeland, John; 1818 list age 68; served in S C line; drew pension in Davidson Co.

Copeland, Richard; 1818 list age 73; served in N C troops; drew pension in Overton Co.

Copeland, Richard Sen; 1840 Census age 81; drew pension in Wayne Co.

Copeland, Westley; 1828 list; served in Wilkinson's 7th reg't inf; drew pension in Wayne Co; (1812).

Copeland, Zaccheus; 1832 list age 70; also 1840 Census; served in N C line; drew pension in Jefferson Co.

Coppinger, Higgins; 1818 list age 96; served in Va line; drew pension in Warren Co.

Copus, William; 1832 list age 87; served in Va line; drew pension in Sullivan Co.

Cornwall, William; 1832 list age 82; served in Va mil; drew pension in Jefferson Co.

Costner, Lucy, widow of Jacob Costner; filed claim for pension in Blount Co abt 1840.

Coulson, David; 1832 list age 84; served in Va line; drew pension in White Co.

Counce, Nicholas; 1832 list age 82; served in N C line; drew pension in Grainger Co.

Courteney, Michael; 1818 list age 73; served in Va line; drew pension in Knox Co; transferred from Jackson Co Ind.

Covey, Samuel; 1832 list age 73; served in N Y mil; drew pension in Knox Co.

Covington, Mathew; 1832 list age 75; served in N C line; drew pension in Carroll Co.

Cowden, Lieut Robert; 1832 list age 80; also 1840 Census; served in N C line; in 1832 he drew pension in Bedford Co; in 1840 he drew pension in Marshall Co; lived with Robert Cowden 3rd.

Cox, Card; 1832 list age 72; also 1840 Census; served in Va line; drew pension in Knox Co.

Cox, Lieut Edward; 1832 list age 75; also 1840 Census; served in Md mil; drew pension in Sullivan Co; in 1840 he lived with John Cox.

Cox, John; 1832 list age 76; also 1840 Census; served in Va mil; drew pension in Roane Co; in 1840 he lived with Samuel Cox.

Cox, Joseph; 1832 list age 73; served in Md mil; drew pension in Sullivan Co.

Cox, Jovan; 1832 list age 73; also 1840 Census; served in N C line; drew pension in McNairy Co.

Cox, Lieut Thomas; 1832 list age 81; also 1840 Census; served in N C mil; drew pension in Sullivan Co; lived with Stephen Miller.

Crab, Benjamin; 1818 list age 76; served in N C troops; drew pension in Wilson Co; d Nov 24 1829.

Crab, Benjamin; 1818 list age 76; served in N C troops; drew pension in Wayne Co.

Crabtree, Isaac; 1832 list age 76; served in Va line; drew pension in Overton Co.

Crabtree, Richard; 1840 Census age 76; drew pension in Campbell Co.

Craig, Alexander; 1832 list age 76; also 1840 Census; served in N C line; drew pension in Henry Co.

Craighead, Robert; served in Davies' Detachment; transferred from N C; drew pension in Knox Co; d May 7 1821.

Crane, Joel; 1832 list age 72; served in N C line; drew pension in Hardeman Co.

Crane, John; 1832 list age 75; served in N C line; drew pension in Stewart Co.

Crane, William; 1832 list age 82; served in N C line; drew pension in Hardeman Co.

Crawford (Crafford) Alexander; 1832 list age 84; served in S C line; drew pension in Maury Co; d 1839.

Crawford, James; 1832 list age 72; served in N C line; drew pension in Haywood Co.

Crawford, Ensign James; 1828 list; drew pension in Maury Co; (1812).

Crawford, James L; 1828 list; served in Tenn mil; drew pension in Maury Co; (1812).

Crawford, John; 1832 list age 72; served in S C line; drew pension in Hamilton Co.

Crawford, Robert; 1832 list age 88; served in S C line; drew pension in Maury Co.

Crawley, Thomas; 1832 list age 79; also 1840 Census; served in Va line; drew pension in White Co.

Creamer, David; 1832 list age 77; served in Md line; drew pension in Greene Co.

Crenshaw, John; 1832 list age 76; served in Va line; drew pension in Roane Co; see Crinshaw.

Creswell, Andrew; 1832 list age 76; served in Va line; drew pension in Sevier Co.

Crew, Robert; 1818 list age 84; served in Va line drew pension in Roane Co; d Feb 2 1834.

Crews, Gideon; 1818 list age 82; served in Va line; drew pension in Knox Co; d Aug 12 1834.

Crews, James; 1840 Census age 86; drew pension in Knox Co.

Crews, Reuben; 1818 list age 70; served in S C line; drew pension in Carroll Co.

Crinshaw, John; 1840 Census age 83; drew pension in Morgan Co; see Crenshaw.

Crisp, John; 1832 list age 79; also 1840 Census; served in Va line;

drew pension in 1832 in Rutherford Co; drew pension in 1840 in Gibson Co; lived with William Crisp.

Criswell, Henry; 1832 list age 75; also 1840 Census; served in S C line; drew pension in Wilson Co; lived with John Criswell.

Criswell, Robert; 1840 Census age 80; drew pension in Wilson Co.

Cross, Abraham; 1832 list age 82; also 1840 Census; served in N C line drew pension in Sullivan Co.

Cross, Elijah; 1832 age 76; also 1840 Census; served in N C mil; drew pension in Sullivan Co; in 1840 he lived with David L Cross.

Cross, William; 1832 list 72; served in N C mil; drew pension in Anderson Co.

Crouch, John; 1840 Census age 84; drew pension in Washington Co; lived with David Mains.

Crow, Thomas; 1818 list age 75; served in S C troops; drew pension in Lawrence Co.

Crownover, Joseph; 1832 list age 73; served in Va line; drew pension in Franklin Co.

Crumb, Peter; 1832 list age 76; also 1840 Census; served in Pa mil; drew pension in 1832 in White Co; drew pension in 1840 in Jackson Co.

Crunk, John; 1818 list age 79; served in N C troops; drew pension in Lincoln Co; transferred from Madison Co Ala.

Crunk, John; 1840 Census age 78; drew pension in Wilson Co.

Crutsinger, Solomon; 1832 list age 82; served in Md line; drew pension in Sullivan Co.

Crye, William; 1832 list age 80; served in S C line; drew pension in McMinn Co; his widow, Sarah Crye, drew pension in Bradley Co, 1840 Census age 78.

Culver, John; 1832 list age 71; served in Pa line; drew pension in Bedford Co.

Cummings, Andrew; 1832 list age 74; served in Pa line; drew pension in Blount Co; his widow, Jane, filed claim for pension in 1843 in Blount Co.

Cummings, Joseph; 1832 list age 72; also 1840 Census; served in Va line; drew pension in White Co.

Cunningham, Andrew; served in 20th reg't inf; drew pension in Knox Co; d in service Apr 25 1815; his heirs were Andrew, James, Robert and John Cunningham; (1812).

Cunningham, James; 1832 list age 74; also 1840 Census; served in Va line; drew pension in McMinn Co; lived with John Cunningham.

Cunningham, John 1832 list age 86; also 1840 Census; served in Va line; drew pension in Warren Co; lived with William Kennard.

Cunningham, Samuel; 1828 list; served in Clarke's 3rd inf; drew pension in Stewart Co; (1812).

Cunningham, Valentine; 1818 list age 79; served in Va line; drew pension in Roane Co; d Oct 17 1832.

Cunningham, William; 1832 list age 85; served in N C line; drew pension in Bedford Co.

Curry, John; 1832 list age 72; served in S C mil; drew pension in Davidson Co.

Curtis, James; 1818 list age 82; served in N C troops; drew pension in Lincoln Co.

Curtis, John; 1832 list age 75; served in Va mil; drew pension in Bledsoe Co.

Curtis, Lieut Joshua; 1818 list age 84; served in N C line; drew pension in Davidson Co.

Curtis, Thomas; 1832 list age 93; served in N C line; drew pension in White Co; his widow Mary Curtis drew pension in 1834 in Nashville Agency.

Cutts, William; drew pension in Knoxville Agency.

Cypert, Robert; 1818 list age 78; also 1840 Census; served in N C troops; drew pension in Wayne Co.

Daimwood, Boston; 1832 list age 81; served in Va line; drew pension in Rutherford Co.

Dale, John; 1832 list age 70; served in Va line; drew pension in White Co.

Dalton, John; 1832 list age 75; served in Va line; drew pension in Bledsoe Co.

Daniel, Benjamin; 1832 list age 87; also 1840 Census; served in N C line; drew pension in Stewart Co.

Daniel, James; 1840 Census age 54; served in Williams' mil reg't; drew pension in Dickson Co; (1812).

Daniel, Jesse; 1828 list; served in West Tenn mil; drew pension in Lincoln Co; (1812).

Darnell, Cornelius; 1832 list age 72; served in Pa mil; drew pension in Lincoln Co.

Darnell, Nicholas; drew pension in Jackson Agency.

Darnell, William; 1832 list age 83; served in N C line; drew pension in Jackson Co.

Darnes, Elizabeth, widow; 1840 Census age 79; drew pension in Smith Co.

Darrow, Benjamin; 1840 Census age 78; served in 1st reg't Conn line; drew pension in Dickson Co.

David, Azariah; 1832 list age 78; served in N C line; drew pension in Rhea Co.

Davidson, Abraham; 1832 list age 79; served in Va mil; drew pension in Humphreys Co.

Davidson, George; 1832 list age 82; served in S C line; drew pension in Dickson Co.

Davidson, John; 1832 list age 75; also 1840 Census; served in N C line; drew pension in Bedford Co.

Davies, John L; 1832 list age 69; served in S C line; drew pension in Wilson Co.

Davis, Anderson; 1840 Census; drew pension in Gibson Co; lived with Benjamin Wickham.

Davis, Andrew; 1832 list age 77; also 1840 Census; served in S C mil; drew pension in Bledsoe Co.

Davis, Asa; 1832 list age 78; served in Va line; drew pension in Maury Co.

Davis, Henry W; 1818 list age 75; served in Va troops; drew pension in Williamson Co.

Davis, James; 1818 list age 57; served in Va troops; drew pension in White Co.

Davis, James; 1832 list age 75; also 1840 Census; served in N C line; drew pension in Hamilton Co.

Davis, Jesse; 1832 list age 77; served in N C line; drew pension in Bedford Co; d Jul 18 1833.

Davis, Joel; 1832 list age 77; also 1840 Census; served in Va line; drew pension in Jefferson Co; d Feb 12 1848.

Davis, John; 1832 list age 75; also 1840 Census; served in N C line; drew pension in Blount Co.

Davis, John; served in 24th reg't inf; drew pension in Sullivan Co; d in service Oct 1814; his heirs were Anna, Mary, and John Davis: (1812).

Davis, Levi; drew pension in Knoxville Agency.

Davis, Nicholas; 1818 list age 70; served in Va line; drew pension in Jefferson Co; d June 16 1818; his widow, Mary Hays Davis, applied for pension Feb 4 1839 while living in Jefferson Co.

Davis, Robert; 1832 list age 84; served in N C line; drew pension in Marion Co.

Davis, Robert C; 1828 list; served in 2nd reg't Mounted Gunmen; drew pension in Wilson Co; (1812).

Davis, Samuel; 1818 list age 77; served in N C troops; drew pension in Warren Co.

Davis, Thomas; 1840 Census age 81; drew pension in Lincoln Co.

Davis, William; 1832 list age 73; served in N J mil; drew pension in Sumner Co.

Davis, William; 1832 list age 75; served in N C mil; drew pension in Monroe Co.

Davis, William 2nd; 1832 list age 72; served in Va mil; drew pension in Cocke Co.

Davison, Brackett; 1828 list; served in Gen Coffee's brig; drew pension in Maury Co; (1812).

Dawson, John; 1818 list age 76; served in Va line; drew pension in Greene Co.

Day, John; 1832 list age 91; served in Va mil; drew pension in Jefferson Co; d Dec 4 1833.

Day, Philip; 1832 list age 71; served in N C line; drew pension in Smith Co.

Deakins, William; 1818 list age 95; served in Pa troops; drew pension in Williamson Co; d Jan 5 1834.

Dean, Richard; 1818 list age 75; served in N C troops; drew pension in Rutherford Co; d Jul 28 1831.

Deldine, Jonathan; 1832 list age 71; also 1840 list; served in N C line; drew pension in Morgan Co; lived with J Deldine.

DeLoach, Simon; 1840 Census age 51; drew pension in Dickson Co; (1812).

Denham, Hernden; 1832 list age 74; served in N C line; drew pension in Jackson Co.

Denham, Washington; 1840 Census age 54; drew pension in Hawkins Co; (1812).

Denkins, Joshua; 1832 list age 72; served in N C line; drew pension in Henry Co.

Denny, David C; 1840 Census age 86; drew pension in Roane Co.

Denny, William; 1840 Census age 47; served in Tenn Mounted inf; drew pension in Smith Co; (1812).

Denton, John; 1840 Census age 81; drew pension in Monroe Co.

Depriest, Robert; 1818 list age 77; served in Va line; drew pension in Claiborne Co.

Dewberry, Andrew; 1832 list age 68; served in N C mil; drew pension in Perry Co.

Dezern, Frederick; 1818 list age 90; served in N C line; drew pension in Hawkins Co.

Dial, Jeremiah; 1832 list age 76; served in S C line; drew pension in Bedford Co.

Dibrell, Charles; 1832 list age 77; served in Va mil; drew pension in Davidson Co.

Dickinson, Nathaniel; 1832 list age 77; served in N C mil; drew pension in Perry Co.

Dickson, Jesse; 1832 list age 80; served in N C line; drew pension in Stewart Co.

Dickson, William; 1840 Census age 54; ·drew pension in Marshall Co; (1812).

Dickson, William; 1832 list age 99; served in N C line; drew pension in Smith Co.

Dill, Archibald; 1832 list age 85; served in N C line; drew pension in Jackson Co.

Dill, Richard; 1832 list age 81; served in N C line; drew pension in Wilson Co.

Dillard, Benjamin; 1832 list age 72; served in Va line; drew pension in Greene Co.

Dillard, John; 1832 list age 82; served in N C line; drew pension in Madison Co; d Jul 10 1833.

Dillom, Henry; 1840 Census; age 80; drew pension in Overton Co; lived with Abraham Grimley.

Dismukes, Paul; 1832 list age 71; served in Va line; drew pension in Jackson Co.

Ditty, John; 1832 list age 79; also 1840 Census; served in Pa line; drew pension in White Co.

Dixon, George; 1818 list age 82; served in Va line; drew pension in Hawkins Co.

Dixon, William; 1828 list; served in Tenn mil; drew pension in Maury Co; (1812).

Dobb, Chesley; 1832 list age 85; served in Va line; drew pension in Claiborne Co.

Dobbins, David; 1832 list age 76; also 1840 Census; served in N C line; drew pension in Maury Co; lived with David D McFalls.

Dobbins, William; 1828 list; served in 1st reg't mounted gunmen; drew pension in Williamson Co; d June 30 1831; (1812).

Dobkins, Jacob; 1832 list age 83; served in Va line; drew pension in Claiborne Co.

Dodd, David; 1818 list age 75; served in N C troops; drew pension in Lincoln Co; d Jan 20 1829.

Dodd, William; 1832 list age 73; also 1840 Census; served in N C line; drew pension in 1832 in McMinn Co; drew pension in 1840 in Bradley Co; lived with George Couch.

Dodson, George; 1840 Census age 79; drew pension in Giles Co.

Dodson, John; 1832 list age 82; served in Va line; drew pension in Hawkins Co.

Doherty, George, Sen; 1832 list age 85; served in Va line; drew pension in Jefferson Co; d May 27 1833.

Dollins, Pressley; 1832 list age 72; served in Va mil; drew pension in Lincoln Co.

Donald, William; 1840 Census age 94; drew pension in Wilson Co where he lived with Thomas Pentecost.

Donelson, Robert; 1832 list age 69; served in N C line; drew pension in Williamson Co.

Dongan, Major James; 1832 list age 80; served in N C mil; drew pension in Franklin Co.

Donnell, William; 1832 list age 74; served in N C line; drew pension in Wilson Co.

Dorse, William; 1832 list age 70; also 1840 Census; served in Va line; drew pension in Fentress Co.

Doss, John; 1818 list age 86; served in Va Continental line; drew pension in Marion Co.

Doss, John, Sen; 1832 list age 92; served in Va mil; drew pension in Jefferson Co; d Dec 4 1833.

Doty, Azariah; 1832 list age 89; also 1840 Census; served in N C line; drew pension in Greene Co; lived with Ephraim Doty.

Dotty (Doty?) Isaac; 1818 list age 84; served in N C troops; drew pension in Overton Co.

Douglass, Edward; 1832 list age 77; served in N C line; drew pension in Jefferson Co.

Douglass, John; 1832 list age 70; also 1840 Census; served in N C mil; drew pension in 1832 in Washington Co; drew pension in 1840 in Sullivan Co.

Douglass, Robert; 1832 list age 76; served in Va line; drew pension in McMinn Co; d Jul 10 1837.

Douglass, Thomas; 1832 list age 75; also 1840 Census; served in N C line; drew pension in Davidson Co.

Douglass, William; 1818 list; served in N C line; drew pension in Davidson Co.

Dove, Thomas; 1832 list age 76; also 1840 Census; served in Va line; drew pension in Knox Co.

Downie, Alexander; 1818 list age 93; served in Md line; drew pension in Blount Co.

Doxey, Jeremiah; 1832 list age 87; also 1840 Census; served on United States Ship Tartar; drew pension in Henderson Co where he lived in 1840 with Stephen H Doxey.

Doyle, John; 1818 list age 86; served in Md line; drew pension in Knox Co.

Drake, Thomas; 1828 list; served in Va line; drew pension in Bedford Co.

Draper, Robert; 1818 list age 87; served in Va line; drew pension in Jefferson Co.

Duboise, Stephen; 1832 list age 75; served in S C line; drew pension in Rutherford Co.

Dudley, Ambrose; 1832 list age 74; served in N C line; drew pension in Carroll Co.

Dudley, Guilford; 1832 list age 78; served in N C line; drew pension in Williamson Co; d Feb 3 1833; his widow Anna Eaton Dudley drew pension in Williamson Co.

Duggan, William; 1840 Census age 49; served in 24th inf; drew pension in Monroe Co; (1812).

Dugger, John; 1832 list age 86; served in Va line; drew pension in Sumner Co.

Dulaney, Benjamin; 1832 list age 77; served in Va line; drew pension in Sullivan Co.

Dulin, William; lived in Smith Co; served in 24th reg't inf; d in service in 1813; his heirs were: Sally, Jane and Jefferson Dulin; (1812).

Dumikin, Daniel; 1818 list age 82; served in Va line; drew pension in Greene Co.

Duncan, Elijah; 1840 Census age 90; drew pension in De Kalb Co.

Duncan, Elijah; 1832 list age 78; served in N C mil; drew pension in Smith Co.

Duncan, John; 1832 list age 84; served in Va line; drew pension in Blount Co.

Duncan, Joseph; 1832 list age 83; served in Va line; drew pension in Washington Co.

Duncan, Thomas; 1832 list age 70; also 1840 Census; served in Va line; drew pension in Monroe Co.

Dunkin (Duncan?) Anthony; 1832 list age 90; served in Va line; drew pension in Greene Co.

Dunlap, James; 1828 list; served in 3rd reg't Tenn mil; drew pension in Monroe Co; (1812).

Dunlap, Josiah; 1818 list age 85; also 1840 Census; served in Va line; drew pension in Greene Co; lived with William Wykle.

Dunlap, Samuel; 1832 list age 76; served in S C line; drew pension in Humphreys Co.

Dunn, William; 1832 list age 82; served in Va line; drew pension in Knox Co.

Durham, Washington; 1828 list; served in Tenn mil; drew pension in Hawkins Co; (1812).

Dyche, Charles; 1832 list age 70; served in Va line; drew pension in Greene Co.

Dycus, Edward; 1832 list age 80; served in N C line; drew pension in Jackson Co.

Dyer, Baldy; served in 39th reg't inf; lived in Davidson Co; d in service Nov 20 1814; his heirs were: Willie, James, William, David, Susanna, Simpson and Mary Dyer; (1812).

Dyer, John; 1840 Census age 80; drew pension in Meigs Co; lived with Robert Pharies.

Dyer, Manoah; 1832 list age 79; served in N C line; drew pension in Campbell Co.

Dysart, John; 1832 list age 84; also 1840 Census; served in N C line; drew pension in 1832 in Bedford Co; drew pension in 1840 in Marshall Co.

Eakin, Samuel; 1832 list age 71; served in N C line; drew pension in Wayne Co.

Eakins, William; 1832 list age 68; served in S C line; drew pension in Bedford Co.

Ealter, John; 1840 Census; drew pension in Rutherford Co.

Ealy, John; drew pension in Jackson Agency.

Earthman, Isaac; 1832 list age 84; served in N C mil; drew pension in Davidson Co.

Easley, Drury; 1828 list; served in 44th reg't inf; drew pension in Sumner Co; (1812).

Ebzey; William; 1818 list age 76; served in Ga line; drew pension in Franklin Co.

Eckleburger, David; 1840 Census age 43; drew pension in Madison Co; lived with Isaac Malett; (1812).

Edding, William; 1832 list age 76; served in N C line; drew pension in Wilson Co.

Edgman, William; 1832 list age 69; served in N C line; drew pension in Roane Co.

Edleman, Michael; 1818 list age 79; served in Md line; drew pension in Greene Co.

Edmondson, William; drew pension in Nashville Agency.

Edwards, Andrew; 1832 list age 81; served in N C line; drew pension in Carroll Co.

Edwards, John; 1832 list age 84; served in Md line; drew pension in Washington Co.

Edwards, William; 1832 list age 82; served in Va line; drew pension in Robertson Co.

Edwards, William; 1832 list age 76; served in N C line; drew pension in Robertson Co.

Egmond, Lot; 1832 list age 74; served in N J line; drew pension in Robertson Co.

Eldridge, Simeon; 1832 list age 76; also 1840 Census; served in N C line; drew pension in 1832 in Roane Co; drew pension in 1840 in McMinn Co.

Elkins, Richard; 1832 list age 73; served in S C line; drew pension in Bedford Co.

Elkins, Shadrach; 1840 Census age 79; drew pension in Lauderdale Co; lived with Robert Walker.

Elliott, Robert; 1828 list; served in 17th reg't U S inf; drew pension in Maury Co; (1812).

Elliot, William; 1832 list age 70; served in S C line; drew pension in Marion Co.

Ellis, Ephraim; 1832 list age 70; served in S C line; drew pension in Jackson Co.

Ellis, Joseph; 1840 Census age 77; drew pension in Grainger Co.

Ellison, Charles; 1832 list age 71; also 1840 Census; served in N C line; drew pension in 1832 in Robertson Co; drew pension in 1840 in White Co.

Embrey (Hembree?) Abraham; 1818 list; served in Va line; drew pension in Cocke Co.

Emert (also given as Emmert) George; 1818 list; also 1840 Census age 83; served in Va line; drew pension in Carter Co; lived with Elizabeth Emert.

Endsley, Deborah, widow; filed claim for pension after 1840 in Blount Co.

Engh, Adam; 1832 list age 81; also 1840 Census; served in Pa line; drew pension in Washington Co; spelled Ingle in Census.

England, Joseph; 1832 list age 71; served in N C line; drew pension in Anderson Co.

Eoff, Isaac; 1832 list age 74; also 1840 Census; served in S C line; drew pension in 1832 in Rutherford Co; drew pension in 1840 in Cannon Co.

Epperson, Thomas; 1832 list age 74; served in N C mil; drew pension in Hawkins Co.

Epley, John; 1840 Census age 78; drew pension in Perry Co.

Eppes, Richard; 1818 list age 62; served in Va line; drew pension in Dickson Co.

Ernest, Felix; 1832 list age 72; served in Va line; drew pension in Greene Co.

Erwin, John; 1832 list age 71; also 1840 Census; served in N C mil; drew pension in Giles Co.

Erwin, Richard; 1840 list age 30; drew pension in Franklin Co; too young for revolutionary service or 1812.

Estes, John; 1832 list age 82; served in Va mil; drew pension in Grainger Co.

Estes, Thomas; 1832 list age 73; served in Va line; drew pension in Lawrence Co.

Estill, Lieut. Wallace; 1832 list age 76; served in Va line; drew pension in Franklin Co.

Etheridge, John; 1818 list age 97; served in N C line; drew pension in Blount Co; he was transferred to West Tenn and retransferred to Blount Co in 1825.

Etter, John; 1828 list; served in Washington's Cav; drew pension in Rutherford Co.

Evans, Andrew; 1832 list age 71; served in Va line; drew pension in Rhea Co.

Evans, Cornelius; 1832 list age 76; served in N C line; drew pension in Sumner Co.

Evans, Gilbert (alias Getree); 1832 list age 75; served in Pa line; drew pension in Greene Co.

Evans, Jane, widow; 1840 list age 72; drew pension in Fentress Co; lived with Thomas Evans.

Evans, John; 1840 Census age 77; drew pension in Lawrence Co; lived with John Evans Jr.

Evans, Joseph; 1818 age 61; served in Va line; drew pension in Claiborne Co.

Evans, Ordin; 1832 list age 78; served in Va line; drew pension in Roane Co.

Evans, Samuel; 1818 list age 71; also 1840 Census; served in Va line; drew pension in Roane Co; lived with L B Davis.

Evans, William; 1828 list; served in Tenn Vol; drew pension in Robertson Co; (1812).

Everett, Robert; 1818 list age 81; served in Va line; drew pension in Blount Co.

Everett, Samuel; 1832 list age 72; served in Md line; drew pension in Carroll Co.

Everett, William; 1832 list age 70; also 1840 Census; served in Va line; drew pension in Marion Co.

Everly, John; 1840 Census age 74; drew pension in Giles Co where he lived with George Everly.

Ewens, Alexander; 1840 Census age 79; drew pension in Marshall Co.

Ewing, Alexander; 1832 list age 72; served in N C line; drew pension in Bedford Co.

Ewing, George; 1832 list age 74; also 1840 Census; served in N C line; drew pension in Blount Co; lived with Samuel McColley.

Ezell, Timothy; 1818 list age 78; served in N C line; drew pension in Giles Co.

Fagg, Joel; 1840 Census age 88; drew pension in Maury Co.

Fagot, John; 1832 list age 71; served in Va line; drew pension in Cocke Co.

Fain, John; 1840 Census age 51; served in Ball's reg't; drew pension in Jefferson Co.

Faire, Jonathan; 1818 list age 82; served in Va troops; drew pension in Smith Co.

Falkner, David; 1832 list age 74; also 1840 Census; served in N C line; drew pension in Knox Co.

Falls, John, 1818 list age 86; served in Pa line; drew pension in Greene Co.

Fancher, Isaac; 1828 list; served in 7th reg't U S inf; drew pension in Overton Co; (1812).

Fane, Charles; 1832 list age 91; served in N C line; drew pension in Bedford Co.

Fann (or Fant) George; 1818 list age 75; served in Va line; drew pension in Greene Co.

Faris, Alexander; 1832 list age 76; served in S C line; drew pension in Obion Co.

Farley, Stephen; 1818 list age 70; served in Va line; drew pension in White Co.

Farris, Caleb; 1832 list age 69; served in S C line; drew pension in Maury Co.

Faulkenburg, David; 1832 list age 86; also 1840 Census; served in S C line; drew pension in 1832 in Rutherford Co; drew pension in Cannon Co; in 1840 he lived with William Pace.

Felkins, John; 1818 list age 74; served in N C line; drew pension in Overton Co.

Felts, Rowland; 1832 list age 79; served in N C line; drew pension in Robertson Co.

Fenner, Ann, widow; 1840 list age 73; drew pension in Madison Co.

Fentress, James; 1832 list age 70; also 1840 Census; served in N C line; drew pension in Montgomery Co.

Fergus, James; 1832 list age 77; served in Pa line; drew pension in Carroll Co.

Fergus, John; 1832 list age 82; served in S C mil; drew pension in Monroe Co.

Ferguson, Isaac; 1840 Census age 83; drew pension in Williamson Co.

Ferguson, James; 1832 list age 75; also 1840 Census; served in N C line; drew pension in Rhea Co; in 1840 he lived with Samuel Ferguson.

Ferguson, John; 1832 list age 75; served in Va mil; drew pension in Franklin Co.

Feris, Isaac; 1832 list age 76; served in S C line; drew pension in Maury Co.

Ferrell, Smith; 1832 list age 76; also 1840 Census; served in N C mil; drew pension in 1832 in Monroe Co; drew pension in 1840 in Overton Co.

Ferrell, William; 1832 list age 77; also 1840 Census; served in N C line; drew pension in Jackson Co.

Field, George; 1828 list; served in Tenn mil; drew pension in Giles Co; (1812).

Fikes, Elisha; 1828 list; served in 2nd reg't Tenn mil; drew pension in Robertson Co; (1812).

Findlay, George; 1832 list age 82; served in N C line; drew pension in Giles Co.

Finn, Peter; 1832 list age 84; served in N C mil; drew pension in Sumner Co.

Fisher, Frederick; 1840 list age 78; drew pension in Marshall Co.

Fisher, John; 1832 list age 77; served in S C line; drew pension in Warren Co.

Fisher, Thomas; 1832 list age 74; served in Va line; drew pension in Robertson Co.

Fite, John; 1832 list age 75; also 1840 Census; served in N J mil; drew pension in 1832 in Smith Co; drew pension in 1840 in DeKalb Co; lived with Henry Fite.

Fite, Leonard; 1832 list age 74; also 1840 Census; served in N J mil; drew pension in 1832 in Smith Co; drew pension in 1840 in De Kalb Co.

Fitch, John; 1832 list age 74; served in Va line; drew pension in Sullivan Co.

Fitzgerald, George; 1818 list age 80; served in Va line; drew pension in Washington Co.

Fleming, Samuel; 1832 list age 77; served in N C line; drew pension in Rutherford Co.

Fletcher, Thomas; 1840 list age 90; drew pension in Hawkins Co; lived with Anthony Smith.

Flewellyn, William; 1832 list age 81; served in N C line; drew pension in Carroll Co.

Flowers, Rowland; served in Va troops; drew pension in Fentress Co; his widow Anna Flowers drew pension in Fentress Co in 1840, aged 78; lived with Archibald Stone.

Floyd, Perry; 1818 list age 76; served in Va line; drew pension in Washington Co; d May 13 1824.

Forbes, Alexander, Sen; 1832 list age 74; also 1840 Census; served in Va line; drew pension in Lincoln Co.

Ford, Ann, widow; 1840 Census age 67; drew pension in Smith Co.

Ford, John C D (alias John D Ford); served in 2nd reg't art; lived in Sullivan Co; d in service Jan 6 1813; his heirs were: Isaac, Hannah, Cromwell and Thomas Ford; (1812).

Ford, John, Sen; 1832 list age 72; also 1840 Census; served in Va line; drew pension in Bledsoe Co.

Ford, Joshua; 1832 list age 77; also 1840 Census; served in Va line; drew pension in Rutherford Co.

Ford, Lloyd; 1832 list age 83; also 1840 Census; served in Va line; drew pension in Washington Co.

Forman, John; 1828 list; served in Tenn mil; drew pension in Jefferson Co; (1812).

Forrest, James; 1832 list age 83; served in N C mil; drew pension in Warren Co.

Forrester, Robert; 1832 list age 76; also 1840 Census; served in Va line; drew pension in 1832 in McMinn Co; drew pension in 1840 in Bradley Co; lived with William Forrester.

Forrester, Stephen; 1832 list age 82; served in N C mil; drew pension in Sumner Co.

Fortune, William; 1832 list age 88; also 1840 Census; served in Md line; drew pension in Sumner Co; lived with Joseph Smith.

Fortner, Ezekial; 1832 list age 74; also 1840 Census; served in N C line; drew pension in Hardin Co.

Foster, John; 1840 Census; drew pension in Henderson Co.

Foster, Richard; served in 24th reg't inf; lived in Rutherford Co; d in service Dec 19 1813; his heirs were: Alcey, Thomas and Mary Foster; (1812).

Foster, William; 1818 list age 67; served in Va line; drew pension in Davidson Co.

Fowler, Sherwood; 1832 list age 74; served in Va line; drew pension in Bedford Co.

Fox, John; 1840 Census age 83; drew pension in Knox Co.

Franklin, Henry; 1818 list age 79; served in Va line; drew pension in Jefferson Co.

Frazier, Alexander; 1832 list age 74; also 1840 Census; served in Pa line; drew pension in Montgomery Co.

Frazier, Henry; 1840 Census age 57; served in 39th reg't U S inf; drew pension in Hawkins Co; (1812).

Frazier, Thomas; 1818 list age 73; also 1840 Census; served in N C line; drew pension in 1832 in Henry Co; transferred from Cumberland Co N C; drew pension in 1840 in Gibson Co.

Frazier, Thomas; 1818 list age 73; served in N C line; drew pension in Hawkins Co.

Frazzle, Nathan; 1832 list age 75; served in S C line; drew pension in Bedford Co.

Freeman, Howell; drew pension in Nashville Agency.

Freeman, John; 1832 list age 71; served in N C line; drew pension in Williamson Co.

Freeman, Zadoc; 1840 Census age 55; drew pension in Washington Co; (1812).

French, Joseph; 1832 list age 74; served in Va mil; drew pension in Fentress Co.

French, Thomas; 1832 list age 79; also 1840 Census; served in N C mil; drew pension in Stewart Co.

Fritz, John; 1832 list age 72; served in Va mil; drew pension in Hawkins Co.

Fry, Gabriel; 1818 list age 74; served in Va line; drew pension in Morgan Co.

Fulkinson, John; 1832 list age 79; served in Va line; drew pension in Washington Co.

Fuller, George, Sen; 1818 list age 77; also 1840 Census; served in N C line; drew pension in Roane Co.

Fuller, Lieut James; 1840 Census age 49; served in 20th inf reg't; drew pension in Jefferson Co; (1812).

Gage, Aaron D; 1832 list age 75; also 1840 Census; served in N J line; drew pension in 1832 in McNairy Co; drew pension in 1840 in Lincoln Co; lived with Easter Westerman.

Gaines, Ambrose; 1832 list age 71; served in Va mil; drew pension in Sullivan Co.

Gains, Anthony; 1818 list age 75; served in N C troops; drew pension in Wilson Co.

Galloway, Michael; 1818 list age 67; served in Md line; drew pension in Sullivan Co; d Dec 17 1827.

Gamble, Thomas; 1818 list age 68; served in Va line; drew pension in Giles Co.

Gamblin, James; 1832 list age 82; also 1840 Census; served in N C line; drew pension in Sumner Co.

Gammon, Harris; 1832 list age 76; also 1840 Census; served in Va line; drew pension in Knox Co; lived with Lewis Gammon.

Gammon, Jesse; 1832 list age 70; also 1840 Census; served in N C line; drew pension in Jefferson Co.

Gann, Nathan; 1832 list age 75; served in N C line; drew pension in Washington Co.

Gann, Thomas; 1832 list age 70; served in N C mil; drew pension in Hamilton Co.

Gann, William, 1828 list; served in 24th reg't U S inf; (1812).

Gardner, John F; 1832 list age 64; served in N C mil; drew pension in Blount Co.

Garland, Elisha; 1832 list age 72; served in N C line; drew pension in Davidson Co.

Garlands, Humphrey; 1818 list age 86; served in N C line; drew pension in Carter Co.

Garrison, John; 1832 list age 76; also 1840 Census; served in S C line; drew pension in Wilson Co.

Garrett, Henry; 1832 list age 80; served in Va line; drew pension in Williamson Co.

Garsage, John; 1832 list age 92; served in N C mil; drew pension in Sullivan Co.

Gaspension, John; 1832 list age 91; served in N C line; drew pension in Anderson Co.

Gass, John, Sen; 1832 list age 75; also 1840 Census; served in N C line; drew pension in Greene Co.

Gates, John, 1832 list age 75; served in Va mil; drew pension in Williamson Co.

Gearran, Solomon; see Geron.

Gent, Charles; 1832 list age 80; also 1840 Census; served in Ga line; drew pension in Robertson Co where he lived with James W Gent.

Gent, Jesse; drew pension in Nashville Agency.

Gentry, Claiborne; 1832 list age 73; served in N C line; drew pension in Davidson Co.

Gentry, David, Sen; 1840 Census age 97; drew pension in Overton Co.

George, Brittain; 1818 list age 94; also 1840 Census; served in N C troops; drew pension in 1818 in Smith Co; drew pension in 1840 in Henry Co.

George, William; 1832 list age 78; also in 1840 Census; served in Va line; drew pension in Lincoln Co.

Geren, Solomon; 1832 list age 73; spelled Gearran in 1840 Census; served in N C line; drew pension in Roane Co.

Gettree, Gilbert; alias Gilbert Evans; 1832 list age 75; served in Pa line drew pension in Greene Co.

Gibbs, John; 1832 list age 78; also 1840 Census; served in Va line; drew pension in Bedford Co; he lived with Ebenezer Gibbs.

Gibson, Billingsly; 1832 list age 84; served in Va line; drew pension in Washington Co.

Gibson, John; 1840 Census age 80; drew pension in Lincoln Co.

Gibson, John; 1818 list age 74; served in Md troops; drew pension in Wilson Co.

Gibson, William; 1840 Census; drew pension in Perry Co.

Gideon, Hogh (Hugh?); 1818 list age 77; served in N C line; drew pension in Franklin Co.

Gilbreath, Thomas; 1818 list age 83; served in Va line; drew pension in Jefferson Co.

Gilham, John; 1832 list age 73; served in S C mil; drew pension in Maury Co.

Gill, George; 1818 list; served in N C troops; drew pension in Wayne Co.

Gillehan, William; 1818 list age 84; served in S C troops; drew pension in Smith Co.

Gilliam, Jacob; 1840 Census age 79; drew pension in Maury Co.

Gillespie, Allen; drew pension in Jonesboro Agency.

Gillespie, Jacob; 1832 list age 81; also 1840 Census; served in Va line; drew pension in Knox Co.

Gillespie, William; 1832 list age 75; served in S C line; drew pension in Haywood Co.

Gilmore, Joseph; 1828 list; drew pension in Davidson Co; transferred from S C; d Feb 23 1825 (1812)

Gist, Thomas; 1832 list age 70; served in Va line; drew pension in White Co.

Given, John; 1840 Census age 76; drew pension in Dyer Co; lived with Alexander McCullock.

Givens, James; 1832 list age 70; also 1840 Census; served in N C mil; drew pension in Gibson Co.

Givens, Patrick; 1818 age 88; served in Pa line; drew pension in Jefferson Co; d Feb 5 1829.

Glasgow, Cornelius; 1832 list age 74; served in N C line; drew pension in Weakley Co.

Glasgow, Richard; 1840 Census age 87; drew pension in Hardeman Co; lived with John Glasgow.

Glen, John; 1818 list age 77; served in Pa line; drew pension in Franklin Co; d Mar 14 1829.

Glenton, John; 1832 list age 73; served in S C line; drew pension in Wilson Co.

Glover, Richard; 1832 list age 78; served in N C mil; drew pension in Sullivan Co.

Goad, William; 1832 list age 80; also 1840 Census; served in Va mil; drew pension in Sullivan Co.

Godfrey, Zachariah; 1828 list; served in 9th inf; drew pension in Roane Co; (1812).

Godsey, Ankey; 1840 Census age 77; drew pension in Sullivan Co; he lived with Jacob Millers.

Godsey, William; 1818 list age 73; served in Va line; drew pension in Sullivan Co; d Feb 7 1831.

Goforth, John; served in 7th reg't inf; drew pension in Jefferson Co; d in service Sept 8 1813; his heirs were: Nancy, Preston, Cornelius and John Goforth; (1812).

Goforth, Zachariah; 1832 list age 74; also 1840 Census; served in N C line; drew pension in Wayne Co; lived with Humphrey Goforth.

Goin, Daniel; 1818 list age 76; served in Va line; drew pension in Campbell Co.

Goins, David; 1832 list age 76; served in Va troops; drew pension in Hamilton Co.

Goings, William; 1818 list age 64; served in Va line; drew pension in Hawkins Co; d Aug 23 1827.

Good, Col Thomas; 1840 Census age 81; drew pension in Tipton Co.

Goodman, Henry; 1832 list age 75; served in S C line; drew pension in Anderson Co; d June 11 1833.

Goodnight, Henry; 1818 list age 75; also 1840 Census; served in N C line; drew pension in Giles Co where in 1840 he lived with David Goodnight.

Goodrich, John, sen; 1832 age 77; served in Va line; drew pension in Davidson Co.

Goodwin, David; 1832 list age 71; served in S C line; drew pension in White Co.

Gordon, Abner; 1840 Census age 82; drew pension in Hawkins Co.

Gordon, Charles; 1832 list age 69; served in N C line; drew pension in Williamson Co.

Gordon, Richard; 1832 list age 68; served in N C line; drew pension in Jackson Co.

Gordon, William; 1832 list age 77; also 1840 Census; served in Va line; drew pension in Maury Co.

Gore, Thomas; 1818 list age 71; served in S C line; drew pension in Bedford Co.

Grace, David; filed claim in Blount Co in 1845.

Graham, Isaac; 1832 list age 84; also 1840 Census; served in N C line; drew pension in White Co; lived with Charles Graham.

Graham, John; 1832 list age 69; served in N C line; drew pension in Henry Co.

Graham, William; 1818 list age 85; served in Va troops; drew pension in Montgomery Co.

Graham, William; 1832 list age 85; served in Va line; drew pension in Anderson Co.

Grant, Alexander; 1832 list age 75; served in S C line; drew pension in Franklin Co.

Grant, David; 1818 list age 75; served in N C line; drew pension in Carter Co.

Grant, James; 1818 list age 80; served in Conn line; drew pension in Campbell Co; d Jan 21 1824.

Grantham; Richard; 1832 list age 79; also 1840 Census; served in N C line; drew pension in Grainger Co.

Graves, Reuben; 1832 list age 73; also 1840 Census; served in Va line; drew pension in Jackson Co.

Gray, James; 1832 list age 76; served in S C line; drew pension in Wilson Co; d Nov 5 1832.

Gray, John; 1832 list age 79; served in N C line; drew pension in Lincoln Co.

Gray, Joseph, see Grey, Joseph.

Gray, Samuel; 1832 list age 82; served in N C line; drew pension in Bedford Co.

Gray, William; 1832 list age 77; served in N C line; drew pension in Wilson Co.

Gray, Zerobabel; 1832 list age 75; served in N C line; drew pension in Davidson Co.

Greacy, John; 1832 list age 75; served in N C line; drew pension in Giles Co.

Green, John; 1832 list age 71; served in N C mil; drew pension in Carter Co.

Green, Marsha; see Meshach Greer.

Green, Nathan; 1832 list age 75; also 1840 Census; served in N C line; drew pension in Henderson Co.

Green, Samuel; 1818 list age 85; served in Pa line; drew pension in Washington Co.

Greene, William; 1832 list age 69; served in Va line; drew pension in Wilson Co.

Greenway, William; 1832 list age 78; served in Va mil; drew pension in Washington Co.

Greer, Meshack; 1832 list age 80; also 1840 Census; served in N C mil; drew pension in Morgan Co.

Greer, Richard; 1832 list age 82; served in Pa line; drew pension in White Co.

Greer, Walter; 1832 list age 75; served in Va mil; drew pension in Overton Co.

Greggs, Robert; 1832 list age 76; served in N C line; drew pension in Henderson Co.

Gregory, Berry; 1832 list age 72; also 1840 Census; served in N C line; drew pension in Smith Co.

Gregory, George; 1832 list age 77; served in N C line; drew pension in Jefferson Co; his widow, Sarah Gregory, drew pension in Hamilton Co.

Gregory, Capt. George; 1840 Census age 61; served in Doherty's Tenn mil; drew pension in Jefferson Co; (1812).

Gregory, William; 1840 Census age 76; drew pension in Smith Co.

Grey, Joseph; 1832 list age 70; also 1840 Census; served in Va line; drew pension in Sullivan Co.

Grier, John; 1840 Census age 79; drew pension in Sullivan Co where he lived with Jacob Crumley.

Griffin, Moses; 1832 list age 77; served in Md line; drew pension in Hickman Co.

Griffith, John; 1832 list age 78; served in N C line; drew pension in Monroe Co.

Griffith, Joseph; 1832 list age 78; served in Va line; drew pension in Morgan Co; d May 20 1833.

Grigg, Lewis; 1832 list age 77; served in Va line; drew pension in Rutherford Co.

Grigsby, Aaron; 1832 list age 82; also 1840 Census; served in United States Navy; drew pension in Giles Co; in 1840 he lived with Amos Grigsby.

Grimes, John; 1832 list; served in Va line; drew pension in Lincoln Co; d Oct 13 1833.

Grimett, Joshua; 1832 list age 68; also 1840 Census; served in Va line; drew pension in Hickman Co.

Grimmar, Jacob; 1832 list age 78; also 1840 Census; served in N C line; drew pension in Williamson Co.

Grimsley, Joseph; 1832 list age 93; served in Va line; drew pension in Sullivan Co.

Groves, Boston; 1832 list age 87; served in N C mil; drew pension in Knox Co.

Groves, Stephen; 1818 list age 68; served in Mass line; drew pension in Knox Co; d Mar 2 1828.

Gulley, John; 1832 list age 96; served in Va line; drew pension in Jackson Co.

Gunn, John, Sen; 1832 list age 72; also 1840 Census; served in Md line; drew pension in Wilson Co.

Gunny, Timothy; 1832 list; served in N C line; drew pension in Fentress Co.

Gunter, Joel; 1818 list age 76; served in N C troops; drew pension in Warren Co; d Aug 22 1829.

Guthrie, Robert; 1832 list age 77; served in Va line; drew pension in Williamson Co.

Gwin, John; 1832 list age 70; served in N C line; drew pension in Carroll Co.

Hackney, Thomas; 1840 Census age 88; drew pension in Montgomery Co; lived with D W Hackney.

Hadden, George; 1832 list age 83; also 1840 Census; served in Va line; drew pension in Blount Co.

Hadley, Capt. Joshua; 1828 list; served in N C line; drew pension in Sumner Co; d Feb 8 1830.

Hale, Amos; 1832 list age 75; also 1840 Census; served in Md line; drew pension in Washington Co.

Hale, Isaac; 1840 Census age 78; drew pension in Humphreys Co.

Hale, John; 1832 list age 80; also 1840 Census; served in Va line; drew pension in Bledsoe Co; Mar 4 1838.

Hale, John; 1818 list age 79; served in N C troops; drew pension in Stewart Co.

Hale, Nathan; 1832 list age 77; served in Md line; drew pension in Giles Co.

Hale, Nicholas; 1832 list age 72; also 1840 Census; served in N C mil; drew pension in Davidson Co.

Hale, William; 1832 list age 82; served in N C line; drew pension in McMinn Co.

Hales, Isaiah; 1832 list age 71; served in N C mil; drew pension in Hickman Co.

Haley, James; 1832 list age 77; also 1840 Census; served in Va line; drew pension in Davidson Co.

Halfacre, George; 1832 list age 76; served in Va line; drew pension in Knox Co.

Hall, Capt. Clement; 1818 list age 71; served in N C line; drew pension in Davidson Co; d Aug 4 1824.

Hall, David; 1832 list age 74; served in N C line; drew pension in Anderson Co.

Hall, John; drew pension in Knoxville Agency; transferred to Jonesboro Agency 1831 (Rev).

Hall, John; 1840 Census age 83; drew pension in Williamson Co.

Hall, Thomas; 1832 list age 76; served in N C mil; drew pension in Knox Co; d Jul 20 1833.

Hambleton, David; 1832 list age 79; also 1840 Census; served in S C line; drew pension in Gibson Co.

Hambleton, Thomas; 1832 list age 77; served in N C line; drew pension in Sumner Co.

Hamby, William; 1832 list age 97; served in Va line; drew pension in Blount Co where he lived with William Dunn.

Hamilton, Herndon; see Harolson, Herndon; name misspelled in Census.

Hamilton, James; 1840 Census; drew pension in Bradley Co.

Hamilton, Joshua; 1832 list age 74; also 1840 Census; served in Va line; drew pension in Sullivan Co.

Hamilton, Thomas; 1832 list age 75; also 1840 Census; served in N C line; drew pension in Rhea Co.

Hammock, John; 1840 Census age 86; drew pension in Grainger Co.

Hammon, Thomas; 1832 list age 75; served in Va line; drew pension in Hawkins Co; d Feb 24 1834.

Hammons, Absolom; 1832 list age 77; served in N C line; drew pension in Sullivan Co.

Hampton, William; 1832 list age 73; served in Va line; drew pension in McMinn Co.

Hancock, David; 1832 list age 72; served in N C line; drew pension in Anderson Co.

Hancock, Joseph; drew pension in Anderson Co; widow was Mary; (Rev).

Hancock, Martin; 1832 list age 73; served in N C line; drew pension in Wilson Co.

Hancock, Stephen; 1832 list age 81; served in Va line; drew pension in Roane Co.

Hancock, William; drew pension in Knoxville Agency.

Hand, Samuel; 1832 list age 73; also 1840 Census; served in S C mil; drew pension in Warren Co; lived with James Hand.

Handlin, Stephen; 1818 list age 67; served in Pa troops; drew pension in Montgomery Co.

Handly, Ensign Samuel; 1832 list age 82; also 1840 Census; served in N C line; drew pension in Franklin Co; lived with John Handly.

Hankins, Abraham; 1832 list age 70; also 1840 list; served in Va mil; in Lincoln Co.

Hankins, James; 1832 list age 81; served in Va mil; drew pension in McMinn Co.

Hanks, Abraham; 1832 list age 70; also 1840 list; served in Va mil; drew pension in Knox Co; also spelled Hawkins.

Hannah, Andrew; 1832 list age 74; also 1840 Census; served in N C line; drew pension in Washington Co.

Harbison, John; 1818 list age 86; served in Va Continental line; drew pension in Blount Co.

Harbison, John; 1818 list age 86; served in Va line; drew pension in Blount Co.

Hardison, John; 1832 list age 70; served in N C mil; drew pension in Robertson Co.

Hardison, James; 1832 list, also 1840 Census age 81; served in N C mil; drew pension in Maury Co.

Hardy, Thomas; 1832 list age 68; also 1840 Census; served in Va line; drew pension in Claiborne Co.

Hargis, William; 1832 list age 72; served in N C mil; drew pension in White Co.

Harman, Adam; 1832 list age 71; also 1840 Census; served in Va line; drew pension in Washington Co.

Harmon, Charles; 1832 list age 71; also 1840 Census; served in Va line; drew pension in 1832 in Overton Co; drew pension in 1840 in Jackson Co.

Harmons (Hammons?), Absolom; 1832 list age 77; served in N C line; drew pension in Sullivan Co.

Harolson, Capt Herndon; 1832 list age 76; also 1840 Census; drew pension in Haywood Co; name misspelled in Census.

Harper, Josiah; 1832 list age 72; served in Va line; drew pension in Smith Co.

Harper, Richard; 1832 list age 71; served in N C line; drew pension in Claiborne Co.

Harper, Thomas; 1818 list age 89; served in Pa line; drew pension in Jefferson Co.

Harper, Wiley; 1828 list; served in 44th U S reg't; drew pension in Dickson Co; (1812).

Harris, Benjamin; 1832 list age 72; served in Va line; drew pension in White Co.

Harris, David; 1818 list age 68; served in Va line; drew pension in Davidson Co; d May 13 1837.

Harris, Edwin; 1832 list age 76; served in N C line; drew pension in Robertson Co.

Harris, Eleanor, widow; applied after 1840 in Blount Co.

Harris, Hugh; 1818 list age 89; also 1840 Census; served in N C mil; drew pension in Washington Co.

Harris, Jonathan; 1832 list age 73; served in N C line; drew pension in White Co.

Harris, Thomas; 1832 list age 80; served in N C mil; drew pension in Gibson Co.

Harris, Thomas; 1832 list age 80; served in N C mil; drew pension in Gibson Co.

Harrison, Gideon; 1832 list age 72; served in Va line; drew pension in Rutherford Co.

Harrison, Joseph; 1818 list age 68; served in N C troops; drew pension in Blount Co.

Harrison, Nathaniel; 1832 list age 76; served in N C line; drew pension in Blount Co.

Harrison, Thomas; 1832 list age 74; served in N C line; drew pension in Franklin Co.

Harrison, William; 1818 list age 70; served in Md line; drew pension in Hawkins Co; d Aug 4 1826.

Harrison, Lieut William; 1818 list age 68; served in N C line; drew pension in Rutherford Co; d June 22 1833.

Hartley, Laban; 1840 Census age 95; drew pension in Williamson Co; lived with Lucurgus McCall.

Harvey, William; 1832 list age 84; served in N C mil; drew pension in Roane Co.

Hasket, John; 1832 list age 82; also 1840 Census; served in N C line; drew pension in Jefferson Co.

Haul, the heirs of Margaret Haul, widow, filed claim in Blount Co in 1845 based on the Rev. service of her husband.

Haun, John; 1832 list age 68; served in S C line; drew pension in McNairy Co.

Hawe, William; 1818 list age 73; served in Md troops; drew pension in Smith Co.

Hawk, Jacob; 1832 list age 76; also 1840 Census; served in Va line; drew pension in Sullivan Co.

Hawk, Michael; drew pension in Monroe Co; (Rev).

Hawkins, Abraham; see Abraham Hankins.

Hawkins, Joseph; 1832 list age 69; also 1840 Census; served in Va line; drew pension in Jackson Co.

Hawkins, Samuel; 1832 list age 98; served in Mass line; drew pension in Hamilton County.

Hawley, Francis; 1832 list age 72; served in Va line; drew pension in Sullivan Co.

Hawley, Robert; drew pension in Knoxville Agency; (Rev).

Hay, George; 1818 list age 92; served in Va line; drew pension in Jefferson Co.

Hayes, Hugh; 1828 list; served in Williamson's reg't mil; drew pension in Wilson Co (1812).

Haygood, William; 1832 list age 79; served in N C line; drew pension in Davidson Co.

Haynes, Benjamin; 1832 list age 86; also 1840 Census; served in Va line; drew pension in Sumner Co; lived with Thomas Haynes.

Haynes, George; 1818 list age 77; served in Va line; drew pension in Carter Co.

Haynes, Jacob; 1832 list age 72; served in N C line; drew pension in Maury Co.

Haynes, James; 1832 list age 74; also 1840 Census; served in Va line; drew pension in Henry Co.

Haynes, John; 1832 list age 73; served in N C line; drew pension in Giles Co.

Haynes, Joseph; 1840 Census age 89; drew pension in Maury Co, lived with Joseph Kennedy.

Hays, John; 1818 list age 78; served in Va line; drew pension in Jefferson Co; d May 5 1833.

Hays, Lieut Robert; served in N C line; drew pension in Davidson Co.

Hays, William; 1818 list age 76; served in Va line; drew pension in Jefferson Co.

Hayse (Hayes?) Robin; 1840 Census age 46; drew pension in Smith Co; (1812).

Hazlet, Rinley; 1828 list; served in 1812; county of residence unknown; transferred to Tenn from Del; papers burned in War Office.

Hearn, John; 1832 list age 77; served in S C line; drew pension in Henry Co.

Heath, John; served in 3rd reg't; lived in Cocke Co; d in service Sept 21 1814; his heirs were: Edith, Nancy and Polly Heath; (1812).

Hedgfroth, John; 1832 list age 72; served in N C mil; drew pension in Rutherford Co.

Hedrick, William; 1832 list age 89; served in Pa line; drew pension in Sevier Co.

Helm, George; 1818 list age 83; also 1840 Census; served in Md line; drew pension in Fentress Co.

Helton, Edward; 1832 list age 72; also 1840 Census; served in Va line; drew pension in White Co; in 1840 he lived with Joseph B. Glenn.

Hembree, Abraham; 1818 list; served in Va line; drew pension in Cocke Co.

Hemphill, Joseph; 1818 list age 71; served in Va line; drew pension in Claiborne Co.

Hemphill, William; drew pension in Pulaski Agency.

Hemrod, Robert; 1818 list age 88; served in Armand's Legion; drew pension in Sullivan Co; d April 6 1828.

Henderson, David; 1840 Census; served in West Tenn mil; drew pension in Lincoln Co; (1812).

Henderson, George; 1840 Census age 81; drew pension in Overton Co.

Henderson, Isaac; 1818 list age 84; served in N J line; drew pension in Claiborne Co.

Henderson, John; 1832 list age 78; served in S C line; drew pension in Roane Co.

Henderson, Meshack; 1832 list age 78; served in N C line; drew pension in Roane Co.

Henderson, Maj Pleasant; 1832 list age 78; also 1840 Census; served in N C line; drew pension in Carroll Co; lived with James M. Henderson.

Henderson, William; 1828 list; served in 29th U S inf; drew pension in Anderson Co; (1812).

Hendricks, Albert; 1832 list age 75; also 1840 Census; served in Md line; drew pension in Sumner Co.

Hendricks, Solomon; 1832 list age 79; also 1840 Census; served in Md line; drew pension in Carter Co.

Henry, David; 1832 list age 81; also 1840 Census; served in Va line; drew pension in Robertson Co.

Henry, Hugh; 1832 list age 84; served in Va line; drew pension in Robertson Co.

Henry, John; 1832 list age 73; served in Va line; drew pension in Jefferson Co.

Henry, John; 1832 list age 72; served in N C line; drew pension in Wayne Co.

Henry, John; 1832 list age 81; served in Va line; drew pension in Cocke Co.

Henry, Robert; 1832 list age 79; served in Pa line; drew pension in Washington Co.

Henry, William; 1832 list age 84; served in Va line; drew pension in Sevier Co.

Henley, John; 1840 Census age 89; drew pension in Jackson Co.

Hensley, Robert; 1832 list age 74; also 1840 Census; served in N C line; drew pension in Hawkins Co; in 1840 he lived with John Hicks.

Hensley, Samuel; drew pension in Jonesboro Agency.

Henwood, Robert; see Robert Hemwood.

Hernden, widow of Reuben Hernden, drew pension in Hamilton Co in 1843 for his Rev service.

Hereden, James; 1832 list age 72; served in Va line; drew pension in Warren Co.

Herod, William; 1832 list age 85; served in Va line; drew pension in Smith Co.

Herron, David; 1832 list age 104; served in Va line; drew pension in White Co.

Hester, William; 1828 list; served in Tenn mil; drew pension in Roane Co; (1812).

Hewitt, Patrick; 1832 list age 83; also 1840 Census; served in Va line; drew pension in White Co; in 1840 he lived with Jonathan Clenny.

Hibbetts, David; drew pension in Nashville Agency.

Hickey, James; 1832 list age 73; served in Va line; drew pension in White Co.

Hickman, Thomas; 1832 list age 71; also 1840 Census; served in Md line; drew pension in Davidson Co.

Hicks, Joel; 1832 list; drew pension in Hawkins Co; later his service was declared fraudulent and pension was stopped.

Hicks, John; 1840 Census age 80; drew pension in Hawkins Co.

Higgenbotham (Higginbotham), William; 1840 Census age 79; served in Va line; drew pension in Perry Co.

Higgins, James, Sen; 1840 Census age 89; drew pension in Giles Co.

Higgins, John; 1832 list age 76; served in Va State troops; drew pension in Wilson Co.

Higginson, Samuel; 1832 list age 91; served in Va line; drew pension in Sumner Co.

Hill, Daniel; 1832 list age 68; also 1840 Census; served in N C line; drew pension in McNairy Co.

Hill, James; 1832 list age 74; served in N C line; drew pension in Blount Co.

Hill, Jonas; 1832 list age 71; served in N C line; drew pension in Franklin Co.

Hill, Robert; 1818 list age 85; served in Va troops; drew pension in Overton Co.

Hill, Thomas; 1832 list age 76; also 1840 Census; served in N C mil; drew pension in White Co; lived with Winkfield Hill.

Hilles, Samuel; 1840 Census age 81; drew pension in Marshall Co; lived with John Hilles.

Hilton, Abram; 1832 list age 80; also 1840 Census; served in N C line; drew pension in Bedford Co.

Hines, James; 1818 list age 96; also 1840 Census; served in Va line; drew pension in Grainger Co.

Hobbs, Thomas; 1832 list age 74; served in Va line; drew pension in Claiborne Co.

Hobson, Lawson; 1840 Census age 86; drew pension in Giles Co.

Hodges, Edward; 1832 list age 79; served in N C line; drew pension in Obion Co.

Hodges, Willis; 1832 list age 87; also 1840 Census; served in N C line; drew pension in Smith Co; name is William in Census.

Hogan, David, sen; 1818 list age 80; served in S C line; drew pension in Giles Co.

Hogan, Edward; 1832 list age 72; served in N C line; drew pension in Henry Co.

Hogg, Lieut Samuel; 1818 list age 70; served in Va troops; drew pension in Smith Co.

Hogh, Gideon; see Hugh, Gideon.

Hogins, Abraham; 1832 list age 75; also 1840 Census; served in N C line; drew pension in Dickson Co; in 1840 he lived with Archibald Hogins.

Holcombe, Maj Philomel; 1832 list age 72; served in Va line; drew pension in Fayette Co.

Holdway, Timothy; 1832 list age 89; served in N C line; drew pension in Jefferson Co.

Holland, William; 1832 list age 71; served in Md line; drew pension in Morgan Co.

Holliday, John; 1832 list age 72; served in Va line; drew pension in Shelby Co.

Holliday, John; 1840 Census age 78; drew pension in Hardeman Co.

Hollis, William; 1832 list; drew pension in Rutherford Co; he was the heir of Capt John Hollis who served in N C line; William Hollis d Aug 27 1832.

Holloway, Billy; 1818 list age 77; served in Va line; drew pension in Blount Co; d Apr 30 1830.

Holloway, John; 1832 list age 75; served in Pa line; drew pension in Morgan Co; his widow, Rebecca Holloway, 1840 Census age 76, also drew pension in Morgan Co; lived with Rachel Holloway.

Holman, Isaac; 1832 list age 82; served in N C line; drew pension in Lincoln Co.

Holmes, Robert; 1832 list age 85; served in Pa line; drew pension in Sumner Co.

Holt, Robert; 1832 list age 78; served in S C line; drew pension in Jackson Co.

Holt, Shadrach; drew pension in Nashville Agency.

Honey, John; 1840 Census age 79; drew pension in McMinn Co.

Honey, John A; alias Acilla; 1818 list age 74; served in A W White's reg't; drew pension in Claiborne Co.

Hood, Jacob; 1818 list age 70; also 1840 Census; served in Pa line; drew pension in 1818 in Carter Co; drew pension in 1840 in Johnson Co; lived with Nancy Morley.

Hood, John; 1840 Census age 78; drew pension in Roane Co.

Hood, John, Sen; 1832 list age 74; served in N C line; drew pension in McNairy Co.

Hood, Morgan; 1832 list age 70; served in N C line; drew pension in Dickson Co.

Hood, Thomas; 1832 list age 76; served in Va mil; drew pension in White Co.

Hook, Willoughby; 1832 list age 84; served in N C line; drew pension in Blount Co.

Hooker, James; 1832 list age 70; served in Va line; drew pension in Davidson Co.

Hooper, Ennis; 1832 list age 85; served in N C line; drew pension in Marion Co; d Feb 4 1833.

Hooper, Jesse; 1832 list age 76; served in Ga mil; drew pension in Davidson Co.

Hooten, Benjamin; 1832 list age 72; served in N C line; drew pension in White Co.

Hooten, Elijah; 1832 list age 81; also 1840 Census; served in N C line; drew pension in 1832 in White Co; drew pension in 1840 in De-Kalb Co; lived with John Reeves.

Hoover, Henry; 1832 list age 79; also 1840 Census; served in Va line; drew pension in 1832 in Fentress Co; drew pension in 1840 in Overton Co.

Hoover, John M; 1832 list age 74; served in Va line; drew pension in Warren Co.

Hope, William; 1832 list age 73; served in N C line; drew pension in Williamson Co.

Hope, William; 1840 Census age 79; drew pension in Shelby Co.

Hopkins, Jesse; 1832 list age 75; also 1840 Census; served in N C line; drew pension in White Co.

Hopper, Harmon; 1932 list age 74; also 1840 Census; served in N C line; drew pension in Claiborne Co; in 1840 he lived with John Hopper.

Horbin, Joshua; 1832 list age 78; served in N C line; drew pension in Warren Co.

Horn, Jeremiah; 1832 age 78; served in N C line; drew pension in Carroll Co.

Horn, Nicholas; 1832 list age 70; served in N C line; drew pension in Knox Co.

Hornley, Robert; 1832 list age 75; served in Va mil; drew pension in Jefferson Co.

Horton, Daniel, Sr; 1832 list age 82; served in N C line; drew pension in Washington Co.

Horton, Howell, 1828 list; served in Eaton's reg't; drew pension in Hamilton Co; transferred from N C; d May 24 1832; (1812).

Horton, Isaac; 1818 list age 75; also 1840 Census; served in Mass troops; drew pension in 1818 in Lawrence Co; drew pension in 1840 in Wayne Co.

Horton, John; 1832 list age 70; served in N C line; drew pension in Greene Co.

Hoss, George; 1832 list age 74; served in N C line; drew pension in Hawkins Co.

Hotchkiss, Jared; 1832 list age 73; served in Conn line; drew pension in Roane Co.

Houk, Michael; 1832 list age 79; served in N C line; drew pension in Monroe Co.

Hounsler, Charles; 1832 list age 89; served in Va line; drew pension in Montgomery Co.

Hourney, Lieut Alfred; 1828 list; served in 44th U S inf; drew pension in Tenn; county unknown (1812).

House, George; 1832 list age 71; also 1840 Census; served in Va mil; drew pension in Greene Co; in 1840 he lived with Washington House.

House, Jacob; 1828 list; served in 44th reg't U S inf; drew pension in Davidson Co; (1812).

Housely, Robert; served in Rev; drew pension in Jefferson Co.

Houston, Archibald; 1818 list age 82; served in N C line; drew pension in McNairy Co.

Houston, Ensign James; 1832 list age 77; also 1840 Census; served in Va mil; drew pension in Blount Co; in 1840 he lived with Robert Tedford.

Houston, John; 1832 list age 71; served in Va mil; drew pension in Blount Co; d Mar 30 1835.

Houston, William; 1832 list age 72; also 1840 Census; served in Va line; drew pension in Greene Co.

Howard, John; 1832 list age 67; also 1840 Census; served in S C mil; drew pension in Morgan Co.

Howell, Benjamin; 1832 list age 81; served in N C line; drew pension in Grainger Co.

Howell, Charles; 1832 list age 74; served in Va line; drew pension in Washington Co.

Hubbard, David; 1828 list; served in Tenn mil; drew pension in Tenn; county unknown; papers destroyed in War Office; (1812).

Hubbard, Peter; 1832 list age 79; served in S C line; drew pension in Montgomery Co.

Huddleston, John; 1828 list; transferred from N C; drew pension in Tenn; county unknown; papers destroyed in War Office; (1812).

Hudgens, Samuel; 1832 list age 78; served in Va line; drew pension in Robertson Co.

Hudgens, William; 1828 list; served in Tenn vol; drew pension in Davidson Co; (1812).

Hudson, James; 1818 list age 71; served in N C troops; drew pension in Wilson Co.

Hudson, John; 1832 list age 81; also 1840 Census; served in Va line; drew pension in Sullivan Co; in 1840 he lived with Hamilton Peavy.

Hudson, Thomas; 1832 list age 72; also 1840 Census; served in Va line; drew pension in Giles Co; in 1840 he lived with John Sandusky.

Hues, Jacob; 1832 list age 81; served in N C line; drew pension in Maury Co.

Huggins, John; 1818 list age 83; served in N C line; drew pension in Davidson Co.

Hugh, Gideon; 1818 age 77; served in N C line; drew pension in Franklin Co.

Hughes, David; 1832 list age 76; also 1840 Census; served in Va line; drew pension in Sullivan Co.

Hughes, Francis; 1832 list age 75; served in N C line; drew pension in Greene Co.

Hughes, Francis; 1832 list age 72; also 1840 Census; served in Va mil; drew pension in Bledsoe Co; lived with Margaret Hughes.

Hughes, John; 1832 list age 82; served in N C line; drew pension in McMinn Co.

Hughes, Peter; 1832 list age 82; served in Va line; drew pension in Sullivan Co.

Hughes, William; 1828 list; served in Tenn vol; drew pension in Weakley Co (1812).

Huline, George; 1832 list age 73; served in S C mil; drew pension in Williamson Co.

Hull, John; 1832 list age 83; served in Va mil; drew pension in Greene Co.

Hull, Joseph; 1832 list age 79; served in N C line; drew pension in Hardeman Co.

Humphreys, David; 1818 list age 88; served in Pa line; drew pension in Carter Co; d June 6 1832.

Humphreys, George; drew pension in Nashville Agency.

Humphreys, U L; served in 10th reg't inf; lived in Davidson Co; d in service June 24 1813; his heir was Sally B Humphreys; (1812).

Humphreys, William; drew pension in Knoxville Agency.

Hungerfort, James; 1818 list age 79; served in Va troops; drew pension in Williamson Co; d Jul 21 1828.

Hunt, James; 1818 list age 75; served in Va troops; drew pension in Rutherford Co.

Hunt, Thomas; 1832 list age 87; served in Md line; drew pension in Wilson Co.

Hurst, Kemp W; served in 35th reg't inf; lived in Maury Co; d in service Feb 9 1815; his heirs were: Sally and Smith W Hurst; (1812).

Hunter, Samuel; 1832 list age 78; served in N C line; drew pension in Smith Co.

Hunter, Thomas; 1832 list age 71; served in S C line; drew pension in Robertson Co; d Feb 27 1834.

Hunter, Thomas; 1832 list age 77; also 1840 Census; served in N C line; drew pension in Blount Co.

Hurt, James; 1818 list age 81; served in Va troops; drew pension in Maury Co.

Hutcheson, David; 1832 list age 79; served in N C line; drew pension in Henry Co.

Hutcheson, David; 1818 last age 77; served in S C troops; drew pension in Maury Co.

Hyde, Irvine; 1832 list age 75; served in Va line; drew pension in Maury Co.

Hyden, William; 1840 Census age 86; drew pension in Washington Co.

Ingh, Adam; 1832 list age 81; also 1840 Census; served in Pa line; drew pension in Washington Co; spelled Engh in 1832 list.

Inge, Joseph; 1818 list age 76; served in Va line; drew pension in Washington Co; d Dec 27 1822.

Inge, Michael; 1818 list; served in Va line; drew pension in Washington Co.

Ingram; William; drew pension in Knoxville Agency.

Ingham, Thomas; 1832 list age 72; served in Va mil; drew pension in Wilson Co.

Iradon, Henry; 1818 list age 63; served in Va troops; drew pension in Williamson Co; d Mar 2 1823.

Isaacs, Samuel; 1832 list age 75; also 1840 Census; served in S C line; drew pension in Lincoln Co.

Ivey, David; 1832 list age 72; also 1840 Census; served in Va mil; drew pension in Williamson Co.

Ivins, John; 1832 list age 83; served in N C line; drew pension in Williamson Co.

Ives, Thomas; 1818 list age 73; served in Va line; drew pension in Knox Co.

Ives, Thomas; 1840 Census age 82; drew pension in Roane Co.

Ivy, David; 1818 list age 64; served in N C line; drew pension in Davidson Co.

Ivy, Henry; 1832 list age 80; served in N C line; drew pension in Jefferson Co; d Jul 27 1834.

Jack, James; 1832 list age 77; served in Va mil; drew pension in Greene Co.

Jackman, Perkinson; 1840 Census age 77; drew pension in Davidson Co.

Jackson, Churchwell; 1832 list age 76; served in N C line; drew pension in Monroe Co.

Jackson, James; 1828 list; served in Hill's mil reg't; drew pension in Tenn but county unknown; transferred from Va.

Jackson, John; 1832 list age 69; served in Va mil; drew pension in Henry Co.

Jackson, Jonathan; 1818 list age 90; served in Va Continental line; drew pension in Washington Co.

Jackson, Joseph; 1840 list age 84; drew pension in Sumner Co.

Jackson, Mark; 1832 list age 92; served in N C mil; drew pension in Maury Co.

Jackson, Obadiah; 1832 list age 75; served in N C line; drew pension in Henry Co.

Jackson, Robert; served in 1st reg't rifles; lived in Cocke Co; d in service June 12 1815; his heirs were: Louisiana, William, George Washington, John and Robert Jackson; (1812).

Jackson, Lieut Samuel; 1832 list age 79; served in Ga line; drew pension in Washington Co; his widow, Elizabeth Jackson, 1840 pension, age 75, drew pension in Washington Co; lived with Alfred Jackson.

Jackson, Vincent; 1840 Census age 95; drew pension in Knox Co; lived with Alexander Blain.

Jackson, William; 1832 list age 70; served in Va mil; drew pension in Wilson Co.

Jackson, William 2nd; 1832 list age 75; served in Va line; drew pension in Wilson Co.

Jackson, William; 1832 list; 1840 Census age 78; served in N C line; drew pension in Franklin Co.

Jackson, William; 1818 list age 84; served in Va line; drew pension in Blount Co.

Jacobs, Edward G; 1832 list age 73; served in Md line; drew pension in Wilson Co.

Jacobs, Joseph; 1832 list age 83; served in N C mil; drew pension in Bedford Co.

James, Aaron; 1832 list age 79; served in Pa mil; drew pension in Dickson Co.

James, John; drew pension in Marion Co; (Rev).

James, John Frederick; 1832 list age 69; served in Md line; drew pension in Grainger Co.

James, Rolling; 1832 list age 72; served in N C State troops; drew pension Campbell Co.

James, William; 1840 age 45; served in Tenn vol; drew pension in Dickson Co; (1812).

Jamison, John; 1832 list age 75; served in N C mil; drew pension in Grainger Co.

Jared, Joseph, Sen; 1832 list age 74; also in 1840 Census; served in Va line; drew pension in Jackson Co.

Jenkins, James; 1832 list age 74; served in S C mil; drew pension in Sevier Co.

Jennings, Edmund; 1832 list age 81; served in Va mil; drew pension in Davidson Co.

Jennings, Peter; 1840 Census age 88; drew pension in Rutherford Co.

Jennings, Royal; 1832 list age 72; served in Va line; drew pension in Grainger Co.

Jennings, William; 1832 list age 74; served in Va line; drew pension in Lincoln Co.

Jewell, William; 1832 list age 91; also 1840 Census; served in Va line; drew pension in Hawkins Co.

Jewell, William; 1832 list age 77; served in N C mil; drew pension in Davidson Co.

Johnson, Abner; 1832 list age 75; also 1840 Census; served in N C mil; drew pension in Maury Co.

Johnson, Abner; 1828 list; served in 39th reg't U S inf; drew pension in Maury Co; (1812).

Johnson, Barnabas; 1832 list age 81; served in N C line; drew pension in Warren Co.

Johnson, Benjamin; 1818 list age 80; served in N C troops; drew pension in Overton Co.

Johnson, Elisha E; 1818 list age 72; served in S C line; drew pension in Giles Co.

Johnson, Enos; 1832 list age 81; served in Va line; drew pension in Hawkins Co.

Johnson, Gideon; 1840 Census age 86; drew pension in Davidson Co where he lived with George Chadwell.

Johnson, Isaac; 1832 list age 73; served in N C line; drew pension in Wilson Co.

Johnson, Isaac; 1832 list age 71; served in Va mil; drew pension in Carroll Co.

Johnson, James; 1832 list age 74; served in N C line; drew pension in Montgomery Co.

Johnson, James; drew pension in Fentress Co; (Rev).

Johnson, James; 1832 list age 78; served in N C mil; drew pension in Knox Co.; transferred to Ind 1834.

Johnson, Moses; 1832 list age 94; served in N C line; drew pension in Hawkins Co.

Johnson, Jesse; 1818 list; served in N C troops; drew pension in Wilson Co.

Johnson, Nathaniel; 1832 list age 78; served in N C mil; drew pension in Bedford Co.

Johnson, Peter; 1818 list age 76; also 1840 Census; served in Va line; drew pension in Anderson Co.

Johnson, Richard; 1832 list age 74; also 1840 Census; served in Va mil; drew pension in Sumner Co; lived with W A Sanders.

Johnson (Johnston), Robert; 1832 list age 75; also 1840 Census; served in Va mil; drew pension in Knox Co.

Johnson, William; 1818 list age 73; served in Va line; drew pension in Hawkins Co; d Nov 16 1833.

Johnson, Zopher; 1832 list age 72; served in Va mil; drew pension in Greene Co.

Johnston, Gideon; 1832 list age 80; served in N C line; drew pension in Williamson Co.

Johnston, John; 1832 list age 82; served in Va mil; drew pension in Smith Co.

Johnston, Martha Allison, widow of John Johnston; drew pension after 1840 in Maury Co.

Johnston, Robert; drew pension in Fentress Co; (1812).

Joiner, Jonathan; 1832 list age 81; served in Ga line; drew pension in Hardeman Co.

Jones, Benjamin; 1832 list age 74; also 1840 Census; served in Va line; drew pension in Smith Co; in 1840 he lived with Simeon Jones.

Jones, Cadwallader; 1832 list age 89; served in Va mil; drew pension in Wilson Co.

Jones, Darling; 1840 Census age 1840; drew pension in Washington Co.

Jones, Daniel, Sen; 1832 list age 77; also 1840 Census; served in N C mil; drew pension in Hawkins Co; lived with Daniel Jones, Jr.

Jones, David; 1832 list age 79; also 1840 Census; served in Va mil; drew pension in Robertson Co.

Jones, David; 1832 list age 71; served in N C line; drew pension in Knox Co.

Jones, David; 1832 list age 69; served in Va mil; drew pension in Henry Co.

Jones, Edward; 1832 list age 77; served in Va mil; drew pension in Sumner Co.

Jones, George; 1818 list age 88; served in Va troops; drew pension in Williamson Co.

Jones, James; 1832 list age 79; also 1840 Census; served in Va line; drew pension in Robertson Co.

Jones, James; 1832 list age 79; served in S C line; drew pension in Marion Co.

Jones, Elizabeth Goodloe, widow of Samuel Jones; drew pension in Maury Co aft 1840.

Jones, John; 1832 list age 75; served in N C mil; drew pension in Marion Co; d Nov 23 1839; widow, Mary Jones, drew pension.

Jones, John; 1832 list age 92; served in N C mil; drew pension in Maury Co.

Jones, John; 1840 Census age 90; drew pension in Giles Co; lived with Hizer Jones.

Jones, John; 1818 list age 82; served in Va troops; drew pension in Lincoln Co.

Jones, John Sen; 1840 Census age 77; drew pension in Claiborne Co.

Jones, Joseph; 1818 list age 79; served in Va line; drew pension in Greene Co; d Apr 22 1826.

Jones, Joseph; 1832 list age 75; also 1840 Census; served in N C mil; drew pension in Giles Co.

Jones, Martin; drew pension in Knoxville Agency; (Rev).

Jones, Morton; 1832 list age 87; also 1840 Census; served in Va mil; drew pension in 1832 in Franklin Co; drew pension in 1840 in Coffee Co.

Jones, Richard; 1818 list age 73; served in Va troops; drew pension in Rutherford Co.

Jones, Richard; 1832 list age 71; also 1840 Census; served in Va mil; drew pension in Giles Co.

Jones, Richard; 1832 list age 63; served in N C mil; drew pension in Rutherford Co.

Jones, Richard; 1832 list age 85; served in Va line; drew pension in Weakley Co.

Jones, Thomas; 1832 list age 72; also 1840 Census; served in N C mil; drew pension in Sullivan Co.

Jones, Westwood A; 1840 Census age 64; drew pension in Haywood Co; lived with James Waddill; (1812).

Jones, William; 1832 list age 72; served in N C line; drew pension in Smith Co.

Jordan, Hezekiah; 1832 list age 72; served in N C line; drew pension in Lincoln Co.

Jordan, John; 1818 list age 76; served in Va line; drew pension in Blount Co.

Justice, Thomas; 1832 list age 69; served in N C mil; drew pension in Bedford Co.

Keeble, Mary, widow of William Keeble; drew pension in Blount Co.

Keel, Richard; 1832 list age 76; also 1840 Census; served in Va troops; drew pension in Rutherford Co.

Keeney, James; served in 7th reg't inf; lived in Jefferson Co; d in service Feb 20 1814; his heirs were: Sally, Ishom, Margaret, Alfred, Betsey and Matilda Keeney; (1812).

Kelly, Allen; 1840 Census; served in 24th reg't U S inf; drew pension in Jefferson Co; (1812).

Kelly, Charles; 1818 list age 85; served in N C line; drew pension in Jefferson Co.

Kelly, Dennis; 1832 list age 75; served in Del line; drew pension in Wilson Co; his widow, Elizabeth Thompson Kelly, drew pension.

Kelly, James; 1832 list age 75; also 1840 Census; served in S C line; drew pension in 1832 in Hickman Co; drew pension in 1840 in Perry Co.

Kelly, Richard; 1832 list age 71; also 1840 Census; served in Va line; drew pension in Carter Co.

Kelly, William; 1832 list age 76; served in S C line; drew pension in McMinn Co.

Kendle, William; 1832 list age 81; served in S C line; drew pension in Sevier Co.

Kendred, Palmer; 1840 Census age 95; drew pension in Lawrence Co; lived with William Ayers.

Kennedy, Andrew; 1828 list; served in N C mil; drew pension in Blount Co.

Kennedy, Andrew; filed claim in Blount Co aft 1840.

Kennedy, James; 1818 list age 81; served in Va troops; drew pension in Wilson Co; d Feb 14 1830.

Kennedy, John; 1818 list age 82; served in Va line; drew pension in Davidson Co; d May 26 1822.

Kennedy, Rachel, widow of Andrew Kennedy; filed claim in Blount Co.

Kennedy, Thomas; 1832 list age 84; served in Va mil; drew pension in Franklin Co.

Kennedy, William; 1832 list age 74; served in S C line; drew pension in Wayne Co.

Kennedy, William; 1840 Census age 85; drew pension in Wilson Co.

Kennon, Oreasley; 1832 age 73; served in N C mil; drew pension in Wilson Co.

Kent, Peter; 1832 list age 74; also 1840 Census; served in Va line; drew pension in Greene Co.

Kerby, William; 1832 list age 75; served in N C line; drew pension in Jackson Co.

Kerr, Joseph; 1832 list age 73; served in N C line; drew pension in White Co.

Kersey, John; 1832 list age 75; also 1840 Census; served in Va line; drew pension in Warren Co; lived with Jonah Duty.

Kesterton, John; 1832 list age 75; also 1840 Census; served in Va line; drew pension in Greene Co.

Key, William; 1832 list age 73; served in Va mil; drew pension in Sumner Co.

Keys (Keyes), Jeremiah; 1840 Census age 43; served in Tenn mil; drew pension in Washington Co; (1812).

Keys, Mathew; 1832 list age 74; served in Va mil; drew pension in Knox Co.

Kilbourne, Benjamin; 1818 list age 68; served in Va line; drew pension in Blount Co; d June 3 1829.

Kilday (Kildai), Henry; served in 24th reg't inf; lived in Greene Co; d in service Dec 19 1813; his heirs were: Sally, Polly, Barsheba, Rebecca, John and Prudence Kilday; (1812).

Kilgore, Charles; 1828 list; served in Campbell's reg't; drew pension in Greene Co; (1812).

Killebrew, Kinchen; 1832 list age 71; served in N C mil; drew pension in Weakley Co.

Killough, Samuel; 1832 list age 71; also 1840 Census; served in S C mil; drew pension in Rutherford Co; spelled Rillough in Census.

Kindle, William; see William Kendle.

Kindred, Thomas; 1832 list age 74; also 1840 Census; served in Va line; drew pension in Morgan Co.

King, Andrew; 1832 list age 81; served in Va line; drew pension in Claiborne Co.

King, Edward; 1818 list age 62; served in S C line; drew pension in Bedford Co.

King, Hugh; 1832 list age 79; also 1840 Census; served in N C line; drew pension in 1832 in Maury Co; drew pension in 1840 in Giles Co.

King, James; 1832 list age 77; served in N C line; drew pension in Henderson Co.

King, John; 1832 list age 76; served in Pa mil; drew pension in Sullivan Co.

King, Philip; 1832 list age 72; served in N C line; drew pension in Warren Co.

King, Thomas; 1832 list age 80; also 1840 Census; served in Pa line; drew pension in Sullivan Co.

King, William; 1840 Census; drew pension in Sullivan Co; lived with Benjamin H King.

Kirkpatrick, Robert; 1832 list age 80; served in S C line; drew pension in Jackson Co.

Kisner, Jacob; 1832 list age 71; served in Va line; drew pension in Gibson Co.

Kitchen, John; 1832 list age 76; served in Va mil; drew pension in Anderson Co.

Kite, John; drew pension in Jonesboro Agency.

Knight, Absolom; 1832 list age 72; served in N C line; drew pension in Humphreys Co.

Knight, James; 1828 list; served in Dale's Tenn mil; drew pension in Williamson Co (1812).

Knight, John; 1832 list age 74; served in N C mil; drew pension in Smith Co.

Knight, Priscilla, widow of Thomas Knight; drew pension in Sumner Co.

Knox, Joseph; 1832 list age 86; served in N C line; drew pension in Rutherford Co.

Knox, Samuel; 1832 list age 81; also 1840 Census; served in S C line; drew pension in Bedford Co; in 1840 lived with William Eoff.

Koonce, Peter; 1840 Census age 75; drew pension in Lincoln Co.

Koonce, Philip 1832 list age 79; served in N C mil; drew pension in Lincoln Co.

Kryster, John; 1818 list age 82; served in Va troops; drew pension in Williamson Co.

Kurtus, John; 1840 Census age 85; drew pension in McMinn Co.

Kuttle, William; 1818 list age 79; served in Va line; drew pension in Blount Co.

Lackey, Thomas; 1818 list age 70; served in Va line; drew pension in Washington Co; d Aug 24 1829; his widow, Elizabeth Lackey, 1840 Census age 80, drew pension in Washington Co; lived with Elizabeth Hundley.

Lain, Charles; 1832 list age 75; served in Va line; drew pension in Roane Co.

Lain, Charles; 1840 Census age 81; drew pension in Bradley Co.

Lain, Gisborn; see Lane, Gisbin.

Lain, Joseph; 1840 Census age 83; drew pension in Bradley Co.

Laird, Nathaniel 1818 list age 77; served in Pa line; drew pension in Bedford Co; d Feb 7 1832.

Landrum, James; drew pension in Knoxville Agency; transferred to Jonesboro Agency 1831; (Rev).

Landrum, John; 1832 list age 72; served in Va mil; drew pension in Greene Co.

Landrum, Thomas; 1832 list age 74; also 1840 Census; served in N C line; drew pension in Roane Co.

Lane, Drury; 1832 list age 79; served in Va mil; drew pension in Rutherford Co.

Lane, Gisbin; 1832 list age 81; also 1840 Census; served in Va mil; drew pension in 1832 in Wilson Co; drew pension in 1840 in Cannon Co; lived with James C Greer.

Lane, Isaac; 1832 list age 74; also 1840 Census; served in Va line; drew pension in McMinn Co.

Lane, James; 1832 list age 88; served in Va line; drew pension in Grainger Co.

Lane, Joseph; 1832 list age 78; served in Va line; drew pension in Roane Co.

Lane, Tidence; 1832 list age 71; served in N C line; drew pension in Jefferson Co.

Lane, Turner, Sen; 1832 list age 72; also 1840 Census; served in Va line; drew pension in White Co.

Lang, Jonathan; see Long, Jonathan.

Langley, John; 1832 age 74; served in S C line; drew pension in Maury Co; d July 27 1834.

Langley, Thomas; served in 7th reg't inf; lived in Washington Co; d in service Nov 30 1814; his heirs were: William, John and Thomas Langley; (1812).

Lanham, Abel; 1832 list age 75; served in N C mil; drew pension in Claiborne Co.

Lanham, Joseph; 1832 list age 78; served in Va line; drew pension in Anderson Co.

Laren, James; 1832 list age 70; served in N C line; drew pension in Hawkins Co.

Large, Joseph; 1840 Census age 84; drew pension in Knox Co.

Large, Joseph; 1832 list age 73; served in N C line; drew pension in Jefferson Co.

Larrimore, Hugh; 1832 list age 74; served in N C mil; drew pension in McMinn Co.

Lasley, John; 1818 list age 80; served in N C troops; drew pension in Sumner Co.

Lassetor, Hardy; 1840 list age 88; drew pension in Cannon Co; lived with Luke Lassitor.

Latimer, Witheral; 1832 list age 77; served in Mass line; drew pension in Carroll Co.

Lauderdale, William; 1832 list age 92; served in Va line; drew pension in Sumner Co.

Lawhorn, William; 1832 list age 70; served in N C line; drew pension in Maury Co.

Lawrence, Jacob; 1832 list age 75; also 1840 Census; served in N C line; drew pension in 1832 in Maury Co; drew pension in 1840 in Marshall Co; lived with John Lawrence.

Laws, Jacob; 1832 list age 74; served in Va mil; drew pension in Hawkins Co; d Sept 5 1833.

Laws, John; 1832 list age 74; served in Va line; drew pension in Smith Co.

Laws, Josiah; 1832 list age 77; served in S C mil; drew pension in Haywood Co.

Lawson, John; 1832 list age 79; served in N C line; drew pension in Morgan Co.

Lawson, Momon; 1840 Census age 95; drew pension in Hawkins Co where he lived with Peter Lawson.

Lawson, Reuben; 1832 list age 74; served in Pa line; drew pension in Monroe Co; d Oct 24 1833.

Lay, Thomas; 1832 list age 71; also 1840 Census; served in N C line; drew pension in Grainger Co.

Layman, Jacob; 1832 list age 75; also 1840 Census; served in Va line; drew pension in Sevier Co.

Lea, Major; 1832 list age 93; served in N C line; drew pension in Claiborne Co.

Leach, William; 1832 list age 73; served in Va line; drew pension in Carroll Co.

Leake, John M; 1832 list age 76; also 1840 Census; served in Va line; drew pension in Rutherford Co.

Leay (or Lee), William; 1818 list age 85; served in Va line; drew pension in Blount Co.

Leckie, William; 1840 Census age 77; drew pension in Rutherford Co.

Ledmon, William; 1840 Census age 67; served in 1st reg't rifles; drew pension in Washington Co; (1812).

Lee, William; see Leay, William.

Legue, Edmund; 1832 list age 74; served in Va line; drew pension in Smith Co.

Lemaster, Joseph; 1818 list age 68; served in Va troops; drew pension in Maury Co; d Aug 10 1826.

Lents, Benjamin; 1832 list age 79; served in N C mil; drew pension in Bedford Co.

Leonard, Frederick; 1818 list age 73; served in Va line; drew pension in Sullivan Co.

Leonard, John; 1818 list; also 1840 Census age 82; served in Va line; drew pension in Hawkins Co.

Leslie, Alexander; 1832 list age 75; served in Va mil; drew pension in Sullivan Co.

Lesley, Peter; 1832 list age 73; served in N C line; drew pension in Davidson Co.

Lesley, Thomas; 1832 list age 74; served in S C mil; drew pension in McMinn Co.

Lester, Alexander; 1832 list age 79; served in Va line; drew pension in Williamson Co.

Leture, Harmon; 1832 list age 79; served in Pa line; drew pension in Sullivan Co.

Levi, Rice; 1832 list age 70; served in Va line; drew pension in Anderson Co.

Levisky, George; 1832 list age 70; served in Va mil; drew pension in Hawkins Co.

Lewallen, Richard; 1832 list age 71; served in Va line; drew pension in Anderson Co; d May 8 1833.

Lewis, James; 1832 list age 78; served in Va mil; drew pension in Franklin Co.

Lewis, Solomon; 1832 list age 83; also 1840 Census; served in N C mil; drew pension in Claiborne Co where he lived with David Rogers.

Light, John; 1832 list age 67; also 1840 Census; served in Va mil; drew pension in Hawkins Co.

Light, Vochal; 1832 list age 71; served in Va mil; drew pension in Sullivan Co.

Lightfoot, Tapley M; 1832 list age 70; also 1840 Census; served in Va line; drew pension in Williamson Co.

Ligon, Joseph; 1840 Census age 84; drew pension in Montgomery Co; lived with Sol Neville.

Ligon, William; 1832 list age 79; served in Va mil; drew pension in Smith Co.

Lilburn, Andrew; 1832 list age 73; served in Va line; drew pension in Washington Co.

Liles, David; 1832 list age 84; served in N C line; drew pension in Roane Co.

Liles, David; 1832 list age 79; served in N C line; drew pension in Carroll Co.

Liles, Robert; 1840 Census age 81; drew pension in Roane Co; lived with Robert D Liles.

Lindsay, Moses; 1832 list age 72; served in S C line; drew pension in Williamson Co.

Liner, Christopher; 1832 list age 71; served in Ga line; drew pension in McMinn Co.

Linn, William; 1818 list age 78; served in S C troops; drew pension in Maury Co.

Lingo, William; 1818 list age 77; served in Del line; drew pension in Maury Co.

Lingo, William; 1840 Census age 44; drew pension in Hardin Co; transferred from N C; (1812).

Lipscomb, Norvell; see Norvell, Lipscomb.

Lisle, Jackson; 1832 list age 72; also 1840 Census; served in N C line; drew pension in Bedford Co.

Lisle, John; 1818 list age 88; served in S C line; drew pension in Anderson Co; d Apr 15 1824.

Littlefield, William; 1832 list age 78; served in S C mil; drew pension in Carroll Co.

Locke, Charles; 1832 list age 82; served in Va mil; drew pension in Wilson Co.

Lockheart, John; 1832 list age 75; also 1840 Census; served in N C line; drew pension in Warren Co; lived with Robert Tate.

Lockridge, James; 1832 list age 77; also 1840 Census; served in S C mil; drew pension in Maury Co.

Lofty, William; 1832 list age 72; served in Va line; drew pension in Cocke Co.

Long, David; 1832 list age 76; also 1840 Census; served in N C mil; drew pension in Maury Co.

Long, George; 1832 list age 76; served in Va line; drew pension in Hawkins Co.

Long, Henry; 1832 list age 70; served in Va line; drew pension in Greene Co.

Long, Jonathan, Sen; 1832 list; also 1840 Census; served in Md line; drew pension in Hawkins Co; spelled Lang in Census.

Long, Nicholas; drew pension in Jefferson Co; (1812).

Long, Richard; 1832 list age 76; also 1840 Census; served in Va line; drew pension in 1832 in Bedford Co; drew pension in 1840 in Marshall Co.

Long, William; 1832 list age 69; served in N C line; drew pension in Henderson Co.

Longley, William; 1832 list age 73; also 1840 Census; served in Va line; drew pension in 1832 in McMinn Co; drew pension in 1840 in Polk Co.

Lorance, Michael; 1832 list age 84; served in N C line; drew pension in Rutherford Co.

Love, Edmund; 1832 list age 75; served in N C line; drew pension in Rhea Co.

Love, Hezekiah; 1832 list age 82; served in S C line; drew pension in Roane Co; d June 11 1833; widow was Nancy Love.

Love, James; 1840 Census age 78; drew pension in Maury Co.

Love, Nicholas; 1832 list age 70; served in Va line; drew pension in Knox Co.

Lovin, James; 1840 Census age 81; drew pension in Hawkins Co; lived with Edmund Lovin.

Lowry, John; 1832 list age 76; served in N C mil; drew pension in Franklin Co.

Loyd, Nicholas; 1832 list age 81; served in N C mil; drew pension in Bedford Co.

Luckey, Hugh; 1832 list age 72; also 1840 Census; served in N C line; drew pension in Fayette Co.

Luna, Peter, Sen; 1832 list age 74; served in N Y line; drew pension in Lincoln Co.

Lusk, John; 1818 age 99; served in N Y troops; drew pension in Warren Co.

Lusk, Joseph; 1832 list age 82; served in N C line; drew pension in McMinn Co.

Lyles, David; 1840 Census age 84; drew pension in Jackson Co. where he lived with Joshua Draper.

Lyman, James; drew pension in Sevier Co. (Rev).

Lytle, Capt William; 1828 list; served in N C line; drew pension in Rutherford Co; (Rev).

Mabin, John; 1832 list age 84; served in N C line; drew pension in Dickson Co.

Mackey, William; 1818 list age 75; served in S C Continental line; drew pension in Blount Co; d Jul 5 1838.

Madding, Chapness; 1832 list age 69; served in Va line; drew pension in Madison Co.

Madding, Daniel; 1832 list age 69; also in 1840 Census; served in Va line; drew pension in Madison Co; lived with Francis Madding.

Madding, Daniel; 1828 list; drew pension in Wilson Co.

Maddox, Jacob; 1832 list age 69; also 1840 Census; served in Va line; drew pension in Jefferson Co.

Maeyer, John; 1818 list age 76; served in Armand's Corps; drew pension in Stewart Co; transferred from Va and the District of Columbia; d Jan 12 1830.

Magee, James; 1832 list age 72; served in Va line; drew pension in Jefferson Co.

Magill, James; 1832 list age 76; served in Va line; drew pension in Greene Co.

Magert, Henry, Sen; 1832 list age 73; also 1840 Census; served in Va line; drew pension in Sullivan Co; lived with Richard Shipley.

Magert, Henry; 1840 Census age 54; drew pension in Sullivan Co; (1812).

Maholland, John; 1832 list age 82; served in N C mil; drew pension in Wilson Co.

Majors, Robert; 1832 list age 73; also 1840 Census; served in N C mil; drew pension in Bedford Co.

Mairs, Elias; 1832 list age 73; served in N C line; drew pension in Warren Co.

Malaby, John; 1832 list age 85; served in N C line; drew pension in Bledsoe Co.

Mallory, Roger; 1832 list age 79; served in Va line; drew pension in Williamson Co.

Mallory, Timothy; 1828 list; served in 5th reg't Ken mil; drew pension in Tenn; county unknown; (1812).

Mallory, William; 1832 list age 83; served in Va line; drew pension in Wilson Co.

Malone, Deloney; 1832 list age 75; served in N C line; drew pension in Sumner Co.

Manis, Seth; 1840 Census age 78; drew pension in Hawkins Co.

Mank, Andrew; 1832 list age 73; served in Va mil; drew pension in Sullivan Co.

Manley, Ancil; 1832 list age 71; served in Va line; drew pension in Anderson Co.

Mann, Ebenezer, 1818 list age 74; served in Va line; drew pension in Hawkins Co; d Aug 25 1832.

Mann, Robert; 1818 age 71; served in Va line; drew pension in Hawkins Co.

Manson, William; drew pension in Knoxville Agency; his widow was Mary; (1812).

Marion, John F; 1832 list age 74; served in N C line; drew pension in Bedford Co.

Marion, Samuel; 1832 list served in Va line; drew pension in Hawkins Co.

Markham, Lewis; 1832 list age 71; served in Va mil; drew pension in Lawrence Co.

Marney, Amos; 1832 list age 74; served in Va line; drew pension in Roane Co.

Mars, Darby; 1828 list; served in Triplett's reg't; drew pension in Knox Co; (1812).

Marsh, Henry; 1832 list age 73; also 1840 Census; served in Va line; drew pension in White Co.

Marshall, Lieut. Dixon; 1818 list age 72; served in N C troops; drew pension in Smith Co; d Aug 22 1824.

Marshall, Ezekial; 1832 list age 77; also 1840 Census; served in Va mil; drew pension in Dixon Co.

Marshall, Francis; 1832 list age 84; served in Va mil; drew pension in Sumner Co.

Martin, John; 1828 list; drew pension in Tenn; county unknown; papers destroyed in War Office; transferred from Va.

Martin, John; 1818 list age 79; served in Va troops; drew pension in Wilson Co.

Martin, Josiah; 1832 list age 77; served in N C line; drew pension in Bedford Co.

Martin, Mathew, Sen; 1832 list age 71; also 1840 Census; served in Va line; drew pension in Bedford Co.

Martin, Pleasant; 1832 list age 78; served in Va line; drew pension in Wilson Co.

Martin, Richard; 1828 list; served in Tenn vol; drew pension in Davidson Co; (1812).

Martin, Rhodeham; 1832 list age 73; served in N C mil; drew pension in Gibson Co.

Martin, Robert; 1832 list age 77; also 1840 Census; served in N C line; drew pension in 1832 in Marion Co; drew pension in 1840 in Hamilton Co; lived with Alexander Martin.

Martin, Samuel; 1832 list age 73; served in S C line; drew pension in Cocke Co.

Martin, Samuel; 1840 Census age 84; drew pension in Fayette Co.

Martin, William; 1840 Census age 81; drew pension in Marshall Co.

Mason, Lieut Caleb; 1832 list; 1840 Census age 87; served in N C troops; drew pension in 1832 in Dickson Co; drew pension in 1840 in Davidson Co; lived with John Davis.

Mason, Edward; 1832 list age 87; served in Va line; drew pension in Knox Co; d Aug 22 1833.

Massengale, Hal; 1840 Census; drew pension in Sullivan Co; his widow, Elizabeth Emmett Massengale, drew pension in Sullivan Co.

Massengale, Michael; 1832 list age 78; served in Va line; drew pension in Grainger Co.

Massey, Henry; 1832 list age 78; served in N C mil; drew pension in Wilson Co.

Massey, John; 1832 list age 69; served in Va mil; drew pension in White Co.

Matheny, William; 1832 list age 77; served in N C mil; drew pension in Henry Co.

Matheny, William; 1840 Census age 96; drew pension in Carroll Co; lived with Peter Matheny.

Mathews, William; 1832 list age 81; served in Va line; drew pension in Warren Co.

Matlock, Henry; 1840 Census age 54; served in Williamson's Tenn reg't; drew pension in McMinn Co; (1812).

Matlock, Richard; 1832 list age 74; also 1840 Census; served in Va line; drew pension in Hawkins Co; lived with George Matlock.

Maury, William; 1832 list age 73; served in Va mil; drew pension in Wilson Co.

Maxwell, John; 1832 list age 68; also 1840 Census; served in N C mil; drew pension in Haywood Co.

Maxwell, William; 1832 list age 78; served in N C line; drew pension in Smith Co.

May, Cassius; 1832 list age 82; served in Pa line; drew pension in Washington Co.

May, Edward; 1818 list age 63; served in Va troops; drew pension in Maury Co; d June 1 1825.

May, George; 1818 list age 92; served in Va line; drew pension in Jefferson Co.

May, John; 1832 list age 73; served in Va line; drew pension in McMinn Co.

May, Thomas; 1840 Census age 78; drew pension in Gibson Co.

May, William; 1832 list age 76; also 1840 Census; served in N C mil; drew pension in Sumner Co; lived with Major May.

May, William; 1832 list age 70; also 1840 Census; served in Va line; drew pension in 1832 in McMinn Co; drew pension in 1840 in Polk Co.

Mayberry, Benjamin; 1818 list age 77; served in N C troops; drew pension in Sumner Co.

Maybourn, John; 1840 Census age 97; drew pension in Dickson Co; lived with Howell Underwood.

Mayes or Mayers, Samuel; 1832 list age 74; also 1840 Census; served in S C line; drew pension in Maury Co.

Mayes, Thomas 2nd; 1832 list age 84; served in N C line; drew pension in Humphreys Co.

Mayfield, Elijah; 1840 Census age 80; drew pension in Hickman Co.

McAdams, John; 1832 list age 71; also 1840 Census; served in N C line; drew pension in Sumner Co.

McAdow (McAdoo), James; 1832 list age 75; served in N C line; drew pension in Wilson Co.

McAnalley, David; 1832 list age 86; served in Va line; drew pension in Grainger Co.

McAllister, William, Sen; 1840 Census age 80; drew pension in Bradley Co. (see William McCallister).

McBee, Israel; 1832 list; also 1840 Census age 79; served in Va line drew pension in Grainger Co.

McBride, Elizabeth Birdsong, widow of John Ramsey (her first husband); drew pension in Monroe Co.

McBride, James; 1832 list age 84; served in N C line; drew pension in Lincoln Co.

McBride, John; 1832 list age 82; served in N C line; drew pension in Williamson Co.

McCabe, Hugh; 1832 list age 77; served in Va mil; drew pension in Maury Co.

McCalla, John; 1818 list age 84; served in Pa line; drew pension in Knox Co.

McCallon, James; 1832 list age 91; served in S C mil; drew pension in Blount Co.

McCallister, William; 1832 list age 72; served in Md line; drew pension in McMinn Co; (see William McAllister).

McCamish, Thomas; 1832 list age 75; served in Va mil; drew pension in Greene Co.

McCampbell, Solomon; 1832 list age 81; served in Va line; drew pension in Knox Co.

McCanless, John; 1832 list age 80; served in N C line; drew pension in Giles Co.

McCann, Joseph; 1832 list age 77; served in S C line; drew pension in Lawrence Co.

McCarrell, John; 1832 list age 97; served in Pa line; drew pension in Stewart Co.

McCarroll, John; 1818 list age 83; drew pension in Smith Co; transferred from Butler Co Ga; d Aug 17 1828; his widow Keziah McCarroll drew pension.

McCaslin, or McCasland, John; 1832 list age 84; also 1840 Census; served in Pa line; drew pension in Davidson Co; lived with Joshua Drake.

McCay, Robert; 1832 list age 72; also 1840 Census; served in N C mil; drew pension in Blount Co.

McClary, Andrew; 1832 list age 79; served in N C mil; drew pension in Claiborne Co; d Nov 23 1833.

McClaskey, Joseph; 1832 list age 78; served in S C mil; drew pension in Lincoln Co.

McClister, James; 1828 list; served in Stewart's Pa reg't; drew pension in Jefferson Co.

McClung, John; 1832 list age 71; also 1840 Census; served in S C line; drew pension in 1832 in Smith Co; drew pension in 1840 in Sumner Co.

McColler, Alexander N, Sen; 1832 list age 75; also 1840 Census; served in S C mil; drew pension in McNairy Co.

McConnell, Emanual; 1832 list age 77; also 1840 Census; served in S C line; drew pension in 1832 in Maury Co; drew pension in 1840 in Marshall Co.

McCorkle, Archibald; 1832 list age 80; also 1840 Census; served in S C line; drew pension in 1832 in Stewart Co; drew pension in 1840 in Henderson Co.

McCormack (McCormick), Joseph; 1832 list age 67; served in N C line; drew pension in Marion Co; transferred to Jackson Co Ala.

McCormack (McCormick), Robert; 1832 list age 72; also 1840 Census; served in N C line; drew pension in 1832 in McMinn Co; drew pension in 1840 in Bradley Co; lived with Lemuel Carpenter.

McCormick, Thomas; drew pension in Knoxville Agency; transferred to Jonesboro Agency 1831; (Rev).

McCoy, Daniel; 1832 list age 83; also 1840 Census; served in Va line; drew pension in 1832 in Franklin Co; drew pension in 1840 in Rutherford Co.

McCoy, John; 1832 list age 82; also 1840 Census; served in N C line; drew pension in Jefferson Co; lived with William McCoy.

McCoy, Robert; see Robert McCay.

McCrary, Hugh; 1832 list age 76; served in N C line; drew pension in Bedford Co.

McCrary, James; 1832 list age 82; served in Va mil; drew pension in Franklin Co.

McCrory, John; 1832 list age 71; served in N C mil; drew pension in Maury Co.

McCrosky, John; 1832 list age 84; served in Va line; drew pension in Sevier Co.

McCullock, John; 1818 list age 91; served in N C line; drew pension in Giles Co.

McCullock, William; 1818 list age 83; served in Va troops; drew pension in White Co.

McCutchin, John; 1840 Census age 87; drew pension in Davidson Co.

McDaniel, Clement; 1832 list age 74; served in Va line; drew pension in Shelby Co.

McDaniel, James; 1832 list age 76; drew pension in Morgan Co.

McDaniel, James; 1840 Census age 82; drew pension in Johnson Co.

McDaniel, Mathias; 1832 list age 85; served in Va line; drew pension in Sumner Co.

McDonald, James; 1818 list age 74; also 1840 Census; served in Armand's Legion; drew pension in 1818 in Carter Co; drew pension in 1940 in Campbell Co.

McDonald, John; 1818 list age 81; served as a musician in Md line; drew pension in Jefferson Co.

McDonald, Michael; see Michael McDowell.

McDonough, Andrew; 1832 list age 74; also 1840 Census; served in N C mil; drew pension in Bledsoe Co; lived with Anna M McDonough.

McDowell, Michael; 1832 list age 87; served in Va line; drew pension in Claiborne Co; the name is McDowell on printed list but it is said that it should be Michael McDonald.

McElroy, Daniel; 1818 list age 83; served in Pa Continental line; drew pension in Hawkins Co.

McElduff, Lieut Daniel; 1828 list; served in U S army; drew pension in Franklin Co; transferred from Ga; (1812).

McElroy, Micajah; 1832 list age 74; served in N C mil; drew pension in Lincoln Co.

McElyea, Patrick; 1840 Census age 91; drew pension in Franklin Co; lived with Arthur Hatchet.

McFadden, Edward; 1832 list age 93; served in S C mil; drew pension in Maury Co.

McFarland, Jacob; 1832 list age 77; served in Pa line; drew pension in Haywood Co.

McFarland, Lieut Robert; 1832 list age 75; served in N C line; drew pension in Jefferson Co.

McFerrin, Samuel; 1832 list age 73; also 1840 Census; served in Va line; drew pension in Hardin Co; lived with Smith D Cooper.

McFerrin, William; 1832 list age 78; also 1840 Census; served in Va line; drew pension in Tipton Co; lived with Collin Campbell.

McGee, Thomas, 1st; 1832 list age 72; served in N C line; drew pension in Montgomery Co.

McGeorge, Thomas; 1832 list age 74; served in Va line; drew pension in Warren Co.

McGill, James; 1840 Census age 83; drew pension in Monroe Co; lived with Harvey McGill.

McGowan, William; 1832 list age 78; served in S C line; drew pension in Henry Co.

McGuire, Alleghany; 1832 list age 77; also 1840 Census; served in Va mil; drew pension in 1832 in Maury Co; drew pension in 1840 in Hardin Co; lived with Halladay McGuire.

McIntosh, Charles; 1832 list age 74; served in N C mil; drew pension in Robertson Co.

McIntosh, Thomas; 1832 list age 78; served in N C mil; drew pension in Stewart Co.

McIntyre, John; 1818 list age 71; served in Va line; drew pension in Anderson Co; d Sept 1822.

McKarney, James; 1832 list age 81; also 1840 Census; served in Va line; drew pension in Blount Co.

McKey, James; 1840 Census age 76; drew pension in Fayette Co.

McKeddy, Thomas; 1832 list age 74; also 1840 Census; served in S C line; drew pension in Rhea Co; in 1840 he lived with William McKeddy.

McKelvey, William; 1832 list age 80; served in S C line; drew pension in Rutherford Co.

McKenney, Samuel; 1832 list age 75; served in Va line; drew pension in Greene Co.

McKensey; John; 1832 list age 76; served in Va line; drew pension in Carroll Co.

McKenzie, Malcomb; 1828 list; drew pension in Humphreys Co; (1812).

McKey, James; 1840 Census age 76; drew pension in Fayette Co.

McKie, Daniel; 1832 list age 74; served in Va line; drew pension in Maury Co.

McKinley, Robert; 1828 list; served in N C line; drew pension in Jackson Co.

McKissack, Thomas; 1828 list; served in Tenn mounted mil; drew pension in Giles Co; transferred from N C; (1812).

McLain, George; 1832 list age 74; served in N C mil; drew pension in Bedford Co.

McLaughlin, Stephen; 1832 list age 74; also 1840 Census; served in N C line; drew pension in Jefferson Co.

McLeod, Abner; 1840 Census age 44; drew pension in Carter Co; (1812).

McLemore, John; 1832 list age 71; also 1840 Census; served in N C mil; drew pension in Knox Co; lived with William McLemore.

McLusky, William; 1832 list age 67; served in S C line; drew pension in Weakley Co.

McMahon, Andrew; 1818 list age 60; served in Va troops; drew pension in Wilson Co.

McMahon, Daniel; 1832 list age 83; served in N C line; drew pension in Williamson Co.

McMahon, John; 1832 list age 79; served in Va line; drew pension in McMinn Co.

McMemamy, Alexander; 1832 list age 75; served in N C line; drew pension in Wilson Co.

McMillan, Joseph; 1832 list age 91; served in S C line; drew pension in Knox Co.

McMinn, Robert; 1832 list age 71; served in N C line; drew pension in Hawkins Co.

McMurty, John; 1818 list age 81; also 1840 Census; served in Pa troops; drew pension in Sumner Co.

McNabb, Elizabeth, widow of David; 1840 Census age 80; drew pension in McMinn Co; lived with William McNabb.

McNabb, William; filed claim after 1840 while living in Blount Co.

McNatt, John; 1832 list age 85; served in Del line; drew pension in Bedford Co.

McNatt, John; 1832 list age 70; also 1840 Census; served in S C line; drew pension in Roane Co.

McNutt, John; 1840 Census age 105; drew pension in Lincoln Co where he lived with Charles McNutt (McNott on one list).

McPeters, Joseph; 1832 list age 75; also 1840 Census; served in N C line; drew pension Morgan Co.

McPheters, Andrew; drew pension in Knoxville Agency; transferred to Ind; (Rev).

McRaimey, 1832 list age 76; served in N C mil; drew pension in Bedford Co.

McRoberts, David; 1818 list age 84; served in Pa line; drew pension in Bedford Co.

McSpadden, Archibald; 1832 list age 84; served in Va mil; drew pension in Monroe Co.

McSpadden, Samuel; 1832 list age 78; also 1840 Census; served in Va line; drew pension in Jefferson Co; lived with Thomas McSpadden.

McSpadden, Thomas; 1832 list age 86; served in N C line; drew pension in Wilson Co; d May 11 1834.

McVey, Eli; 1818 list age 71; served in S C line; drew pension in Hawkins Co.

McWhater, Aaron; 1832 list age 73; served in N C line; drew pension in Lincoln Co.

Meaden, Andrew; 1832 list age 79; served in N C line; drew pension in Jefferson Co.

Meaderis, Capt John; 1828 list; served in N C line; drew pension in Bedford Co.

Meadors, Daniel; 1832 list age 70; served in N C mil; drew pension in Bedford Co.

Meador, Isom; 1832 list age 73; served in Va mil; drew pension in Smith Co.

Meadors, Joel; 1832 list age 75; served in Va mil; drew pension in Smith Co.

Means, John; filed claim in Blount Co after 1840.

Medley, John; 1832 list age 88; served in Va line; drew pension in White Co.

Medlin, Bradley; 1832 list age 75; also 1840 Census; served in N C mil; drew pension in 1832 in Wilson Co; drew pension in 1840 in Madison Co; lived with Eaton Lenusford.

Meeks, Alexander; 1832 list age 69; served in Va line; drew pension in Lincoln Co.

Menably, Michael; 1818 list age 86; served in Va line; drew pension in Blount Co.

Merriam, Francis; 1818 list; served in Va line; drew pension in Knox Co; d Aug 12 1822.

Merris, John; 1818 list age 71; served in Pa line; drew pension in Blount Co.

Metcalf, William; 1832 list age 67; served in N C line; drew pension in Marion Co.

Miars (Myers?), Elias; 1840 list age 83; drew pension in Carroll Co; he lived with William Stoker.

Midkiff, Josiah; 1832 list age 74; served in Va line; drew pension in Grainger Co.

Milburn, Thomas; 1832 list age 92; served in Va line; drew pension in Sumner Co.

Milburn, William; 1832 list age 81; served in Va line; drew pension in Greene Co.

Miles, A; 1840 Census age 91; drew pension in Rutherford Co where he lived with Patterson Miles.

Miles, Jacob; 1832 list age 78; served in N C mil; drew pension in Robertson Co.

Miles, Leonard; 1832 list age 73; served in Pa line; drew pension in Lincoln Co.

Miles, Thomas, Sen; 1832 list age 81; served in Va line; drew pension in Wilson Co.

Millen, John; drew pension in Knoxville Agency; (Rev).

Miller, Adam; 1832 list age 73; also 1840 Census; served in S C line; drew pension in Roane Co.

Miller, Frederick; 1832 list age 73; also 1840 Census; served in N C line; drew pension in Carroll Co.

Miller, Henry; 1832 list age 74; served in N C line; drew pension in Jackson Co.

Miller, James; 1832 list age 85; served in Va mil; drew pension in Claiborne Co.

Miller, James; drew pension in Nashville Agency.

Miller, John; 1832 list age 67; served in N C mil; drew pension in Gibson Co.

Miller, John; 1832 list age 73; also 1840 Census; served in Va mil; drew pension in Carter Co.

Miller, John B; 1832 list age 73; also 1840 Census; served in Va line; drew pension in Sumner Co; lived with J B Miller.

Miller, John H; 1840 Census age 77; drew pension in White Co.

Miller, John H; 1832 list age 99; served in Va mil; drew pension in Knox Co.

Miller, Mark; 1840 Census age 75; drew pension in Fayette Co where he lived with Jefferson Miller.

Miller, Mark; 1828 list; served in Tenn mounted mil; drew pension in Giles Co; (1812).

Miller, Martha, a widow; filed claim in 1845 in Blount Co.

Miller, Martin; 1832 list age 74; served in N C line; drew pension in Claiborne Co; d Aug 29 1838.

Miller, Samuel; buried in the National Cemetery in Chattanooga with the words "Soldier of the Revolution" on his tombstone; he was put on the pension roll July 9 1814; served in the 39th U S Infantry; appears in the 1828 list marked county unknown; served in the War of 1812 as well as the Rev.

Milliken, James; 1832 list age 80; served in N C line; drew pension in Cocke Co.

Mills, Gideon; 1828 list; served in 1st reg't rifles; drew pension in Davidson Co; d May 29 1829; (1812).

Mills, Hardy; 1832 list age 71; served in N C line; drew pension in Hawkins Co.

Milstead, Zelus; 1832 list age 78; served in Va mil; drew pension in Lincoln Co.

Milton, John; drew pension in Knoxville Agency; (Rev).

Milton, Nathaniel; 1832 list age 75; served in N C line; drew pension in Morgan Co.

Milum, Jordan; 1832 list age 84; also 1840 Census; drew pension in Hickman Co.

Minton, Ebenezer; 1818 list age 74; served in Va line; drew pension in Blount Co; transferred from Lee Co Va.

Mitchell, James; 1832 list age 69; also 1840 Census; served in N C mil; drew pension in Maury Co.

Mitchell; James; 1832 list age 80; served in Va line; drew pension in Robertson Co.

Mitchell, John; 1832 list age 74; served in N C mil; drew pension in Maury Co.

Mitchell, Mark; 1818 list age 81; served in Va troops; drew pension in Warren Co.

Mitchell, Solomon; 1832 list age 74; served in S C line; drew pension in Hawkins Co.

Mitchell, Solomon; 1832 list age 73; served in N C line; drew pension in Sumner Co.

Mitchell, William; 1832 list age 73; also 1840 Census; served in N C line; drew pension in Rutherford Co.

Molsbey, William, Sen; 1832 list age 75; also 1840 Census; served in Va line; drew pension in Hawkins Co.

Mond, William; 1818 list age 74; served in Va line; drew pension in Roane Co.

Monday, William; 1832 list age 71; served in S C line; drew pension in Claiborne Co.

Montgomery, James; 1840 Census 49; served in 39th reg't U S inf; drew pension in Monroe Co; (1812).

Montgomery, Jonathan; 1840 Census age 75 served in N C mil; drew pension in Carroll Co.

Month, Ambrose; 1832 list age 69; served in Va line; drew pension in Knox Co.

Moore, George; drew pension in Knoxville Agency.

Moore, Henry; 1832 list age 74; served in N C mil; drew pension in Bedford Co.

Moore, James; 1832 list age 71; served in N C line; drew pension in Hawkins Co.

Moore, James; 1832 list age 84; served in N C line; drew pension in Montgomery Co.

Moore, James; 1832 list age 83; served in Pa line; drew pension in Rutherford Co.

Moore, John; 1840 Census age 77; drew pension in Haywood Co.

Moore, John, Sen; 1832 list age 73; also 1840 Census; served in N C mil; drew pension in Bedford Co.

Moore, Randolph; 1832 list age 76; drew pension in Bedford Co.

Moore, Robert; 1832 list age 71; also 1840 Census; served in N C line; drew pension in McNairy Co; lived with Janey Moore.

Moore, Samuel; 1832 list age 72; also 1840 Census; served in N C line; drew pension in White Co.

Moore, Susan Mitchell, widow of Elijah Moore; drew pension in Sumner Co.

Moore, Thomas; 1832 list age 103; served in N C line; drew pension in Rhea Co.

Moore, Thomas; 1840 Census age 78; drew pension in White Co.

Moore, William; 1832 list age 75; also 1840 Census; served in Va line; drew pension in 1832 in Monroe Co; drew pension in 1840 in Roane Co; lived with James Moore.

Moore, Lieut Col William; served in N C mil; drew pension in Smith Co; d Dec 1823.

Mooreland, Thomas; 1832 list age 81; served in Pa line; drew pension in Monroe Co.

Moreland, Charles; 1832 list age 70; also 1840 Census; served in Va mil; drew pension in Carter Co; lived with Wright Moreland.

Morgan, Benjamin; 1832 list age 72; also 1840 Census; served in Va mil; drew pension in Davidson Co.

Morgan, Gideon; 1840 Census age 65; served in 26th reg't; drew pension in Monroe Co; (1812).

Morgan, James; 1840 Census age 81; drew pension in Marion Co.

Morgan, John; drew pension in Nashville Agency.

Morgan, John; 1818 list age 74; served in Pa line; drew pension in Greene Co.

Morgan, Thomas, Sen; 1832 list age 83; also 1840 Census; served in Va line; drew pension in Greene Co.

Morgan, Valentine; 1832 list age 73; served in N C line; drew pension in Grainger Co.

Morrell, Thomas; 1832 list age 73; also 1840 Census; served in N C line; drew pension in Sullivan Co.

Morris, Abner; see Abner Norris; 1832 list is wrong as the pension documents give the name Abner Norris.

Morris, Lester; 1832 list age 71; also 1840 Census; served in Va line; drew pension in Giles Co; lived with T A Westmoreland.

Morris, Seth; 1840 Census age 78; drew pension in Hawkins Co.

Morris, William; 1832 list age 73; also 1840 Census; served in N C mil; drew pension in Sumner Co.

Morris, William; 1818 list age 82; served in N C line; drew pension in Grainger Co.

Morrisat, Joseph; 1828 list; served in 24th reg't U S inf; drew pension in Hawkins Co; (1812).

Morrison, James; 1818 list; also 1840 Census age 86; served in Va line; drew pension in Hawkins Co.

Morrison, John; 1832 list age 69; also 1840 Census; served in N C line; drew pension in Bedford Co.

Morrison, John; 1832 list age 77; also 1840 Census; served in Va line; drew pension in Greene Co.

Morrison, William; 1832 list age 84; served in S C line; drew pension in Jefferson Co.

Morrison, William; 1832 list age 75; served in N C line; drew pension in Dickson Co.

Morrow, John; 1828 list; served in Tenn mil; drew pension in Franklin Co; (1812).

Morton, Thomas; drew pension in Jonesboro Agency.

Morton, Thomas; 1840 Census age 45; drew pension in Gibson Co; (1812).

Morton, William; 1832 list age 74; served in Va line; drew pension in Gibson Co.

Moseley, James; 1818 list age 74; served in Va line; drew pension in Bedford Co.

Mosier, Abraham; see Mozier, Abraham.

Mosier, Francis; 1832 list age 72; served in Md line; drew pension in Monroe Co.

Motheral, Henry; 1832 list age 77; served in N C line; drew pension in Wilson Co.

Mowry, Peter; 1832 list age 74; served in Va line; drew pension in Knox Co.

Moyers, Peter; 1832 list age 82; served in Pa mil; drew pension in Lincoln Co.

Mozier, Abraham; 1832 list age 78; served in N C mil; drew pension in Anderson Co; d Oct 22 1836.

Mullagen, John; 1832 list age 80; served in N C line; drew pension in Hickman Co.

Mullen, Jacob; 1832 list age 75; served in Pa line; drew pension in Franklin Co; d Nov 4 1833.

Mullins, Anthony; 1828 list; served in Washington's Cav; drew pension in Lincoln Co; (1812).

Mullins, Flower; 1832 list age 75; also 1840 Census; served in N C mil; drew pension in Hawkins Co.

Mullins, Joseph; 1832 list age 95; served in Va mil; drew pension in Bedford Co.

Murphey, Daniel; 1840 Census age 78; drew pension in Henderson Co where he lived with Daniel H Murphey.

Murphey, Bartholomew; 1832 list age 75; also 1840 Census; served in N C line; drew pension in Perry Co.

Murphey, Edward; 1832 list age 92; served in Va line; drew pension in McMinn Co.

Murphey, John; 1832 list age 74; served in N C line; drew pension in Jefferson Co.

Murphey, William; 1832 list age 74; also 1840 Census; served in N C line; drew pension in Jefferson Co; lived with Samuel Box.

Murray, James; 1840 Census age 88; drew pension in Bedford Co.

Murrell, Benjamin; 1832 list age 74; served in Va mil; drew pension in Weakley Co.

Myers, Thomas; 1832 list age 72; served in N C mil; drew pension in Lincoln Co.

Myrick, Mathew; 1832 list age 82; also 1840 Census; served in N C line; drew pension in Henry Co; lived with William Myrick.

Narramore, John; 1832 list age 72; also 1840 Census; served in S C line; drew pension in Bledsoe Co.

Nall, Richard; 1832 list age 71; also 1840 Census; served in N C line; drew pension in Hickman Co.

Nash, William; 1832 list age 71; served in N C line; drew pension in Dyer Co.

Neace, Martin, Sen; 1840 Census age 82; drew pension in Henry Co.

Neal, Zephania; 1832 list age 81; served in Va line; drew pension in Wilson Co.

Neel, John; 1832 list age 80; served in N C mil; drew pension in Blount Co.

Neely, George; 1832 list age 72; served in S C line; drew pension in Williamson Co; d Mar 18 1833.

Neely, John; 1818 list age 94; served in Va line; drew pension in Knox Co.

Nelms, John E; 1832 list age 80; served in N C mil; drew pension in Hardeman Co.

Nelson, Elizabeth, widow; filed claim in Blount Co in 1849.

Nelson, Hance; 1832 list age 70; served in N C mil; drew pension in Knox Co.

Nelson, Jarrett; 1818 list age 64; served in Va line; drew pension in Davidson Co.

Nelson, John; 1832 list age 80; also 1840 Census; served in N C line; drew pension in 1832 in Warren Co; drew pension in 1840 in Coffee County.

Nelson, John; 1832 list age 77; served in N C mil; drew pension in Knox Co.

Nelson, Moses; 1840 Census age 41; served in Indian campaigns; drew pension in Hamilton Co.

Nelson, William; 1832 list age 87; served in N C line; drew pension in Hawkins Co.

Nelson, William; 1828 list; served in Tipton's company U S army; drew pension in Washington Co; (1812).

Nesbit, John, Sen; 1832 list age 78; also in 1840 Census; served in N C mil; drew pension in Dickson Co; lived with Allen Nesbit.

Nesbit, Robert, Sen; 1840 Census age 80; drew pension in Dickson Co.

Nestor, Frederick; 1832 list age 94; served in N C mil; drew pension in Campbell Co.

Nevill, Thomas; 1832 list age 73; served in Va mil; drew pension in Rutherford Co.

Nevill, Yelverton; 1832 list age 70; also 1840 Census; served in N C mil; drew pension in Jackson Co.

New, William; 1832 list age 72; served in N C mil; drew pension in Wilson Co.

Newan (Newman?), John; 1828 list; served in Elbert's reg't; drew pension in Robertson Co; transferred from Va; (1812).

Newberry, James; 1828 list; served in Sparks' U S company; drew pension in Sumner Co; (1812).

Newman, Jacob; 1832 list age 85; served in Pa mil ;drew pension in Knox Co.

Newman, Jacob; 1832 list age 72; also 1840 Census; served in Pa mil; drew pension in Jackson Co; lived with Catherine Murphey.

Newman, Joseph; 1840 list age 81; drew pension in Rutherford Co; lived with Joseph Nesbit.

Newson, William; 1832 list age 73; served in Va mil; drew pension in Maury Co.

Newton, Abraham; drew pension in Jackson Agency.

Nimley, Henry; 1832 list; age 72; served in Va line; drew pension in Anderson Co.

Nichols, Charles; 1828 list; served in Campbell's reg't; drew pension in Greene Co.

Nixon, John; 1818 list age 71; served in Va line; drew pension in Knox Co.

Nolen, Shadrach; 1832 list age 82; also 1840 Census; served in S C line; drew pension in Hardin Co.

Noline, James; 1832 list age 79; served in S C line; drew pension in Madison Co.

Norman, William; 1832 list age 71; also 1840 Census; served in Va line; drew pension in McMinn Co.

Norris, Abner; 1832 list age 75; served in Va troops; also in N C troops; drew pension in White Co; the name is Morris in 1832 list but Abner Norris in the pension documents.

Norsworthy, James; 1818 list age 65; served in N C line; drew pension in Bedford Co.

Northern, Solomon; 1818 list age 82; drew pension in Blount Co; transferred from Wayne Co Ky.

Norton, Alexander; 1832 list age 75; served in Va line; drew pension in Blount Co; d Oct 1835.

Norton, George; 1818 list age 81; served in Md line; drew pension in Hawkins Co; d Dec 25 1823.

Norvell, Lieut Lipscomb; 1840 Census age 84; served in 3rd reg't Va line; drew pension in Davidson Co; lived with James Walker.

Nucom, Julius; 1818 list age 61; served in Va line; drew pension in Sullivan Co; d Jan 1 1820.

Nucom, Solomon; 1818 list age 74; served in Va line; drew pension in Sevier Co; d Feb 18 1834.

Null, John; drew pension in Blount Co; (Rev).

Nun, Thomas; 1832 list age 83; also 1840 Census; served in Va line; drew pension in Claiborne Co; lived with Sarah Larcham.

Nunelee, Edward, 1832 list age 78; served in Va line; drew pension in Hickman Co.

Nunn, Whorton; 1840 list age 85; drew pension in Claiborne Co; lived with Henry Nun.

Oakley, Susan, widow; 1840 Census age 82; drew pension in Wilson Co.

Obar, Robert; 1818 list age 76; served in N C line; drew pension in Rhea Co.

Oglesby, Elisha; 1832 list age 75; served in Va mil; drew pension in Sumner Co.

Oliver, Douglass; 1840 list age 88; drew pension in Anderson Co.

Ollis, Boston; 1832 list age 90; served in S C mil; drew pension in Morgan Co.

O'Neal, Darius; 1840 Census age 76; drew pension in Cocke Co.

O'Rear, Daniel; 1832 list age 75; served in Va line; drew pension in Franklin Co.

Orsborne, Nathaniel; 1840 Census age 89; drew pension in Roane Co; lived with Elizabeth Burk.

Orr, James; 1818 list age 84; served in N C line; drew pension in Bedford Co; transferred from Caldwell Co Ky.

Orr, Joshua; 1832 list age 73; served in Va mil; drew pension in Fayette Co.

Ostean, David; 1840 Census age 79; drew pension in Bedford Co.

Ousley, John; 1832 list age 77; also 1840 Census; served in Va line; drew pension in Claiborne Co.

Overby, William; 1832 list age 79; served in N C line; drew pension in Carter Co.

Overton, Eli; 1832 list age 74; served in N C mil; drew pension in Hawkins Co.

Owen, Bailey; 1832 list age 76; also 1840 Census; served in N C mil; drew pension in Fentress Co.

Owen, Frederick; 1832 list age 82; served in Va mil; drew pension in Davidson Co.

Owens, James; 1832 list age 72; served in S C mil; drew pension in Robertson Co.

Owens, John; 1832 list age 73; served in Va mil; drew pension in Smith Co.

Owsley, John; see Ousley.

Paine, Edmund; drew pension in Pulaski Agency.

Palmer, John; 1832 list age 78; served in Ga line; drew pension in Henry Co; his widow, Susannah Palmer, was 77 in 1840 when she drew pension in Henry Co; lived with John L. Palmer.

Palmer, Thomas; 1832 list age 73; also 1840 Census; served in Va mil; drew pension in 1832 in Cocke Co; drew pension in 1840 in Hamilton Co.

Pamplin, William; 1832 list age 72; also 1840 Census; served in Va mil; drew pension in Lincoln Co; lived with Henry Pamplin.

Pannel, John; 1840 Census age 49; served in 27th Regt; drew pension in Monroe Co; (1812).

Panter, Edom; 1832 list age 100; served in Va line; drew pension in Washington Co; name is Adam Panter in ms list of Knoxville Agency.

Parham, Lewis; 1840 Census age 55; drew pension in Marshall Co; (1812).

Parker, Abraham; 1832 list age 66; also 1840 Census; served in N C line; drew pension in Maury Co.

Parker, Peter; 1832 list age 77; served in N C mil; drew pension in Stewart Co.

Parker, Richard; 1840 list age 55; drew pension in Sullivan Co; (1812).

Parker, Thomas; 1840 Census age 85; drew pension in Obion Co.

Parker, Thomas; 1832 list; served in Va line; drew pension in Hardin Co.

Parker, Timothy; 1832 list age 74; also 1840 Census; served in N C line; drew pension in Rutherford Co.

Parks, James; 1828 list; served in Isaac's reg't mil; drew pension in Blount Co; transferred from N C; d April 21 1832.

Parr, John; 1818 list age 75; served in N J line; drew pension in Roane Co.

Parrish, Robert; 1832 list age 78; served in Ga mil; drew pension in Williamson Co.

Parrish, Thomas; 1832 list age 74; also 1840 Census; served in N C mil; drew pension in Sumner Co.

Parson, George; 1818 list age 73; also 1840 Census; served in Va line; drew pension in 1818 in Greene Co; drew pension in 1840 in Sevier Co.

Parsons, Thomas; 1818 list age 69; served in Va line; drew pension in Anderson Co; d Feb 15 1825.

Passmore, David; 1832 list age 73; served in N C mil; drew pension in Dickson Co.

Patten, Jacob; 1832 list age 70; also 1840 Census; served in Va line; drew pension in Monroe Co.

Patten, Joseph; 1832 list age 72; also 1840 Census; served in N C line; drew pension in Morgan Co.

Patten, Thomas; served in 25th U S inf reg't; drew pension in Bedford Co; (1812).

Patterson, Robert; 1832 list age 77; also 1840 Census; served in S C line; drew pension in Giles Co.

Patterson, Thomas; 1832 list age 74; served in Va line; drew pension in Davidson Co.

Patterson, Williams; 1832 list age 80; served in Va line; drew pension in Morgan Co.

Patterson, William; 1840 Census age 87; drew pension in Anderson Co.

Patton, John; 1832 list age 78; served in S C line; drew pension in Bedford Co.

Paugh, Young; 1832 list age 81; served in Va line; drew pension in Marion Co.

Pawns, James; 1832 list age 68; name is Pond in 1840 Census; served in S C mil; drew pension in Sumner Co; lived with Mary Rice.

Payne, Charles; 1832 list age 76; served in Va mil; drew pension in Warren Co.

Payne, John; 1832 list age 79; served in Va line; drew pension in Sumner Co.

Peak, Abel; 1832 list age 74; also 1840 Census; served in Va line; drew pension in Morgan Co.

Peary, Thomas; 1832 list age 76; served in N C line; drew pension in Rutherford Co.

Pearson, Abel; 1832 list age 70; also 1840 Census; served in Va line; drew pension in White Co; in 1840 he lived with Joseph Cummings.

Pearson, Charles; 1832 list age 72; also 1840 Census; served in Va line; drew pension in 1832 in Franklin Co; drew pension in 1840 in Coffee Co.

Pearson, David; 1832 list age 82; served in Va line; drew pension in Rutherford Co.

Pearson, Sterling; 1840 Census age 87; drew pension in Coffee Co; lived with Ellis Pearson.

Peary, George; 1832 list age 77; served in N. C mil; drew pension in Williamson Co.

Peck, Able; drew pension in Knoxville Agency; (Rev).

Peck, Peter; 1832 list age 68; also 1840 Census; served in N C mil; drew pension in Claiborne Co.

Pelham, William; 1832 list age 80; served in S C line; drew pension in Warren Co.

Pemberton, Joseph; 1818 list age 57; served in Pa. line; drew pension in Davidson Co; d June 21 1822.

Perkins, John; 1840 Census age 77; drew pension in Hardin Co; lived with James Saxon.

Perkins, John (alias Thomas Carson); 1832 list age 69; served in Va mil; drew pension in Franklin Co.

Perkins, Moses; 1832 list age 76; served in Ga mil; drew pension in Warren Co.

Perkins, Thomas Hardin; drew pension in Nashville Agency.

Perkins, William; served in Hazen's reg't; drew pension in Hawkins Co; (1812).

Perrigen; Hollister; 1818 list age 61; served in Va troops; drew pension in White Co.

Perrin, Nathan; 1832 list age 72; served in Mass line; drew pension in Sullivan Co.

Perry, Daniel; 1828 list; served in Long's reg't; drew pension in Monroe Co; transferred from N C.

Perry, Jesse; 1832 list age 79; also 1840 Census; served in N C line; drew pension in Knox Co; lived with Lewis Perry.

Perry, John; 1832 list age 73; served in N C line; drew pension in Roane Co.

Perry, Nicholas; 1832 list age 74; served in N C line; drew pension in Madison Co.

Perryman, John; 1832 list age 71; served in Va line; drew pension in Fayette Co.

Persons, Benjamin P; served in Tenn mil; 1840 list age 58; drew pension in Montgomery Co; (1812).

Peters, William; 1832 list age 74; also 1840 Census; served in N C line; drew pension in McMinn Co; lived with George Monroe.

Peterson, Daniel; 1818 list age 83; served in Pa line; drew pension in Greene Co.

Petters, Thomas; served in 24th U S inf; drew pension in Bedford Co; transferred from Va; (1812).

Petty, John; 1818 list age 76; also 1840 Census; served in N C line; drew pension in 1818 in Hawkins Co; drew pension in 1840 in Jefferson Co; lived with William T Allerson.

Petty, Thomas; 1840 Census age 76; drew pension in Benton Co.

Petty, Thomas; 1832 list age 69; served in N C line; drew pension in Dickson Co.

Phillips, Bennett; 1832 list age 70; served in N C mil; drew pension in Rutherford Co.

Phillips, Clemmon; 1832 list age 71; served in N C line; drew pension in Morgan Co.

Philips, David; 1832 list age 79; served in N C mil; drew pension in Jackson Co.

Phillips, George; 1828 list; served in 2nd reg't N C line; drew pension in Monroe Co; d Oct 24 1828.

Philips, John; 1818 list age 74; served in N C troops; drew pension in Lawrence Co; d Sept 7 1828.

Philips, Joseph; 1832 list age 81; served in Va line; drew pension in Claiborne Co; d Apr 22 1833.

Philips, William, Sen; 1840 Census age 91; drew pension in Overton Co.

Pickens, Andrew; 1832 list age 85; served in S C line; drew pension in Maury Co.

Pickens, Andrew; 1832 list age 81; also 1840 Census; served in Va line; drew pension in Fayette Co; lived with J S Pickens.

Pierce, Capt James; 1832 list age 86; served in N C line; drew pension in Washington Co; d Apr 1 1833.

Pierce, John; 1832 list age 77; also 1840 Census; served in Va line; drew pension in Hawkins Co.

Pierce, Joshua; 1818 list age 79; served in Md line; drew pension in Washington Co.

Pierce, Capt Joshua; 1832 list age 77; also 1840 Census; served in Md line; drew pension in Williamson Co.

Pillow, Col William; 1828 list; served in 2nd Tenn vol; drew pension in Maury Co; (1812).

Pinn, David; 1840 Census age 80; drew pension in Knox Co; lived with Lutida Dabney.

Pistole, Charles, Sen; 1832 list age 77; served in Va line; drew pension in Maury Co.

Pitt, Henry; 1832 list age 74; also 1840 Census; served in N C line; drew pension in Sumner Co.

Plant, John; 1840 Census age 56; drew pension in Humphreys Co; (1812).

Poindexter, Chapman; 1832 list age 74; also 1840 Census; served in Va line; drew pension in Grainger Co.

Pollard, Chatten D; 1840 Census age 79; drew pension in Bledsoe Co.

Pond, James; see James Pawns.

Pool, Ephraim; 1832 list age 78; served in 'S C line; drew pension in Montgomery Co; his widow Lucinda Pool, drew pension in 1840, age 75; lived with John Pool.

Poore, Thomas; 1818 list age 70; served in N C troops; drew pension in Hickman Co.

Pope, Philip; 1840 list age 78; drew pension in Smith Co.

Porter, Charles; 1832 list age 73; served in Md line; drew pension in Washington Co.

Porter, James; 1818 list age 81; served in Pa troops; drew pension in Smith Co.

Porter, Mitchell; 1832 list age 75; served in Va mil; drew pension in Sevier Co.

Porterfield, Richard; 1840 Census age 82; drew pension in Knox Co.

Porterfield, Richard; 1818 list age 70; served in Va line; drew pension in Greene Co.

Portwood, Page; 1832 list age 86; also 1840 Census; served in Va mil; drew pension in Anderson Co.

Posey, Harrison; 1828 list; served as fifer in 24th reg't inf; drew pension in Claiborne Co; (1812).

Postley, John; 1832 list age 72; served in N C line; drew pension in Hawkins Co.

Potter, James; 1832 list age 75; served in Va troops; drew pension in Cocke Co.

Potts, James; 1832 list age 77; served in N C line; drew pension in Williamson Co.

Potts, William; 1832 list age 68; served in S C line; drew pension in Henry Co.

Powell, Abraham A; 1832 list age 77; served in Va line; drew pension in Wilson Co.

Powell, William; 1840 Census age 74; drew pension in Henry Co.

Pratt, Thomas; 1818 list age 75; served in N C line; drew pension in Hawkins Co.

Pressley, Andrew; 1840 Census age 90; drew pension in Caliborne Co; lived with Squire J Harper.

Presley, John; 1832 list age 84; served in N C line; drew pension in Monroe Co.

Prewett, Reuben; 1818 list age 73; also 1840 Census; served in Va troops; drew pension in Sumner Co.

Price, Anjer; 1818 list age 77; served in Va troops; drew pension in Warren Co.

Price, James; 1818 list age 74; served in Va line; drew pension in Knox Co.

Price, James; 1818 list age 74; served in Va line; drew pension in Knox Co.

Price, John; 1818 list age 76; served in Va line; drew pension in Greene Co.

Price, Reece; 1832 list age 83; served in N C mil; drew pension in McMinn Co.

Price, Royal; 1832 list age 70; served in N C line; drew pension in Morgan Co.

Price, Thomas; 1840 Census age 70; drew pension in Hawkins Co.

Price, William; 1832 list age 72; served in N C line; drew pension in White Co.

Pridemore, Jonathan; 1832 list age 76; served in Pa line; drew pension in Hawkins Co.

Priestley, Charles; 1832 list age 87; served in S C line; drew pension in Morgan Co.

Prim, James; 1832 list age 78; served in N C mil; drew pension in Wilson Co.

Proctor, William; 1832 list age 85; served in Md line; drew pension in Sumner Co.

Pruett, Hansom; 1818 list age 76; served in N C troops; drew pension in Wilson Co.

Pryor, Mathew, Sen; 1832 list age 75; served in N C line drew pension in Marion Co.

Puckett, John; 1832 list age 69; also 1840 Census; served in Va mil; drew pension in 1832 in White Co; drew pension in 1840 in De Kalb Co.

Puckett, Josiah; 1818 list age 82; also 1840 Census; served in Va troops; drew pension in 1818 in Montgomery Co; transferred from Ky; drew pension in 1840 in Humphreys Co.

Pullen, John; 1832 list age 69; served in Va line; drew pension in Sumner Co.

Purkinson, Jackson; 1832 list age 69; served in Va line; drew pension in Wilson Co.

Purviance, Joseph; 1840 Census age 78; drew pension in Henderson Co.

Putty, William; 1832 list age 84; served in Va mil; drew pension in Wilson Co.

Quarles, Francis; 1832 list age 82; served in Pa line; drew pension in Knox Co.

Queener, John; 1832 list age 73; served in Md line; drew pension in McMinn Co.

Rackley, Micajah; 1818 list age 76; served in N C troops; drew pension in Smith Co.

Ragains, Thomas; 1832 list age 83; served in N C line; drew pension in Williamson Co.

Ragin, Owen; 1832 list age 72; served in N C mil; drew pension in Sumner Co.

Ragsdale, Baxter; 1832 list age 74; served in Va line; drew pension in Bedford Co.

Ragsdale, Benjamin; 1832 list age 75; also 1840 Census; served in N C line; drew pension in Williamson Co.

Raidinger, Samuel; 1832 list age 75; served in Pa line; drew pension in Warren Co.

Rainey, Isaac; drew pension in Nashville Agency.

Rainey, John; 1832 list age 77; served in N C line; drew pension in White Co.

Rainey, John; 1832 list age 84; served in S C mil; drew pension in Bedford Co.

Rains, John; 1832 list age 79; served in Va line; drew pension in Carter Co.

Rains, John; 1840 Census age 81; drew pension in Hawkins Co.

Rains, John; 1832 list age 75; served in N C line; drew pension in Bledsoe Co; his widow, Letitia Rains, 1840 Census age 71.

Ramsey, Daniel; 1832 list age 69; also 1840 Census; served in N C line; drew pension in Jackson Co.

Ramsey, James; 1828 list; served in Armand's corp; drew pension in Rutherford Co.

Ramsey, James, Sen; 1818 list age 79; served in Va line; drew pension in Franklin Co.

Ramsey, Robert; 1832 list age 75; also 1840 Census; served in N C line; drew pension in Henry Co.

Randolph, Henry; 1832 list age 77; also 1840 Census; served in Va line; drew pension in Fayette Co; lived with Samuel Morgan.

Raney, John; 1840 Census age 84; drew pension in McMinn Co.

Range, Jonathan; applied in Carter Co, July 5 1842 for pension of his father, James Range, which was allowed.

Rankhorn, Joseph; 1832 list age 74; also 1840 Census; served in N C line; drew pension in 1832 in Warren Co; drew pension in 1840 in DeKalb Co.

Rankin, Robert; 1832 list age 75; also 1840 Census; served in N C line; drew pension in McNairy Co.

Rankin, Robert; 1832 list age 86; served in N C mil; drew pension in Gibson Co.

Rankin, William; 1832 list age 76; served in N C mil; drew pension in Greene Co; d Dec 13 1833.

Rape, Gustavus; 1832 list age 70; also 1840 Census; served in S C mil; drew pension in Dickson Co.

Rawlings, William; 1832 list age 69 served in S C mil drew pension in Franklin Co.

Raye, Samuel; 1832 list age 81; served in N C line; drew pension in Jefferson Co.

Reace, Mary; 1840 Census age 23; drew pension in Rhea Co.

Read, John; 1832 list age 72; served in S C line; drew pension in Campbell Co.

Reader, Benjamin; 1840 Census age 80; drew pension in Overton Co; lived with John Walker.

Reagan, Larkin; 1832 list age 87; also 1840 Census; served in N C line; drew pension in Franklin Co.

Reagen, Darby; 1832 list age 77; served in Ga line; drew pension in Monroe Co.

Reams, Bartley; alias Barclay Rheams; served in 7th reg't inf; lived in Jefferson Co; d in service Mar 10 1815; his heirs were: Richard D, David, Obediah, Elizabeth, Anna and Jaers Reams; (1812).

Reams, Jesse; 1832 list age 76; served in Va mil; drew pension in Stewart Co.

Rector, Maxmillian; 1818 list age 76; also 1840 Census; served in Va line; drew pension in McMinn Co.

Rector, Uriah; 1818 list age 78; served in Va line; drew pension in Roane Co.

Redding, William H; 1840 Census age 81; drew pension in Lawrence Co.

Reed, Abraham; 1832 list age 79; served in Va troops; drew pension in Monroe Co.

Reed, Isaiah; 1832 list age 75; served in N C mil; drew pension in Maury Co.

Reed, John; 1832 list age 70; served in N C line; drew pension in Bedford Co.

Reed, Joseph; 1828 list; served in Cleveland's reg't; drew pension in Knox Co.

Reed, Josiah; 1840 Census age 84; drew pension in Gibson Co.

Reed, Lovett; 1832 list age 79; served in N C line; drew pension in Bledsoe Co; his widow was Libbie Reed.

Reese, Charles T; 1828 list; served in Tenn vol; drew pension in Davidson Co; d 1830; (1812).

Reeves, Samuel; 1818 list age 81; served in N C troops; drew pension in Lincoln Co.

Reid, David; 1832 list age 74; served in Pa line; drew pension in McMinn Co.

Reid, William; 1840 Census age 75; drew pension in Hamilton Co; lived with James Roy.

Reynolds, Aaron; 1832 list age 80; served in Va line; drew pension in Giles Co; d Apr 16 1833.

Reynolds, Ezekial; 1832 list age 74; also 1840 Census; served in N C line; drew pension in Bedford Co; in 1840 he lived with Michael Reynolds.

Reynolds, Henry; 1832 list age 77; served in Va mil; drew pension in Greene Co.

Reynolds, Jacob; 1840 Census age 47; served in 39th inf; drew pension in Franklin Co; (1812).

Reynolds, Jethro; served in 1st reg't rifles; lived in Roane Co; died in service; date of death not given; his heirs were: Alfred, Nancy, Polly, Calvin, Keziah, Cynthia and Jacob Reynolds; (1812).

Reynolds, Samuel; 1832 list age 77; also 1840 Census; served in S C line; drew pension in Franklin Co.

Reynolds, Thomas; 1828 list; served in Johnson's mil; drew pension in Williamson Co; (1812).

Reynolds, William; 1832 list age 71; served in S C line; drew pension in Dickson Co.

Rhea, John; served in 24th reg't inf; lived in Rhea Co; d in service Dec 9 1813; his heirs were: Jenney, Sarah, Elizabeth and Nancy Rhea; (1812).

Rhea, Lunar; served in 39th U S inf; drew pension in Warren Co; (1812).

Rhea, Robert; 1828 list; served in Johnson's Tenn reg't; drew pension in Monroe Co; (1812).

Rhea, Robert; 1832 list age 71; also 1840 Census; served in Va line; drew pension in 1832 in Knox Co; drew pension in 1840 in Blount Co.

Rhodes, Alexander drew pension in Jackson Agency.

Rich, Jacob; 1832 list age 72; served in N C line; drew pension in Franklin Co.

Richards, James; 1828 list; served in Tenn vol; drew pension in Wilson Co; (1812).

Richards, Stephen; 1840 Census age 75; drew pension in Gibson Co; lived with Patrick Gleason.

Richardson, Amos; drew pension in Rhea Co; (Rev).

Richardson, James; 1832 list age 72; served in N C line; drew pension in Rhea Co.

Richardson, John; 1832 list age 74; served in N C line; drew pension in Overton Co.

Richie, James; 1832 list age 79; served in Va mil; drew pension in Wilson Co.

Richey, Peter; 1832 list age 73; served in N C line; drew pension in Jackson Co.

Rider, Reuben; 1832 list age 80; served in Va line; drew pension in Wilson Co.

Ridley, George; 1828 list; served in Tenn vol; drew pension in Williamson Co; (1812).

Riggins, James; 1832 list age 79; also 1840 Census; served in N C line; drew pension in McMinn Co.

Riggs, Reuben; 1832 list age 87; served in N C line; drew pension in Giles Co.

Riggs, Samuel; 1832 list age 74; also 1840 Census; served in N C line; drew pension in Hawkins Co.

Riley, John; drew pension in Knoxville Agency.

Rillough, Samuel; see Samuel Killough.

Richie, Alexander; 1832 list; drew pension in Claiborne Co.

Roach, James; 1832 list age 76; served in Va line; drew pension in Wilson Co; d Jan 29 1834.

Roach, John; 1832 list age 74; served in Va mil; drew pension in Montgomery Co.

Roark, Michael; 1832 list age 74; served in N C line; drew pension in Hawkins Co; his widow Letitia Roark drew pension in 1840; the name is spelled Rork on one list.

Roberts, Edmund; 1832 list age 77; also 1840 Census; served in N C line; drew pension in McMinn Co.

Roberts, Joshua; 1832 list age 73; served in Va line; drew pension in Morgan Co.

Roberts, Mark R; 1828 list; served in Tenn vol; drew pension in Hardeman Co; (1812).

Roberts, Reuben, Sen; 1818 list age 79; also 1840 Census; served in N C troops; drew pension in Warren Co.

Roberts, Thomas; 1832 list age 95; served in Va line.

Roberts, William; 1832 list age 72; served in N C line; drew pension in Hamilton Co.

Robertson, Jesse; 1818 list age 75; served in N C troops; drew pension in Montgomery Co.

Robertson, John; 1832 list age 89; served in Md line; drew pension in Madison Co.

Robertson, Joseph; 1832 list age 74; served in N C line; drew pension in Blount Co.

Robertson, Thomas; 1832 list age 72; served in Va line; drew pension in Monroe Co.

Robertson, William; 1832 list age 76; served in Va line; drew pension in Sevier Co.

Robins, John; 1832 list age 78; served in N C line; drew pension in Henderson Co.

Robinson, James; 1818 list age 81; served in Pa line; drew pension in Blount Co.

Robinson, John; 1832 list age 72; served in N C line; drew pension in McNairy Co.

Robinson, Richard; 1840 Census age 104; drew pension in Lawrence Co; lived with Catherine Brown.

Robinson, Samuel; 1832 list age 73; served in S C line; drew pension in Hardin Co.

Robinson, William; drew pension in Nashville Agency.

Rock, John; 1818 list age 81; served in Pulaski's and Armand's Legions; drew pension in Washington Co.

Rodgers, John A; drew pension in Knoxville Agency.

Rogers, Benjamin; 1832 list age 79; served in Va line; drew pension in Campbell Co; his widow, Martha Rogers, 1840 Census age 75; lived with William A Rogers.

Rogers, Charles; 1828 list; served in Tenn mil; drew pension in Davidson Co; d Oct 6 1824; (1812).

Rogers, Daniel; 1840 Census age 72; drew pension in Henry Co.

Rogers, Jeremiah; 1832 list age 69; served in Va line; drew pension in Marion Co.

Rogers, Joseph; 1832 list age 84; served in S C line; drew pension in Bedford Co.

Rogers, Ralph; 1832 list age 74; served in S C line; drew pension in Jackson Co.

Rogers, Samuel; 1832 list age 71; served in N C line; drew pension in Henry Co.

Rogers, William; drew pension in Nashville Agency.

Rogers, William; 1832 list age 94; served in Va line; drew pension in Hamilton Co.

Rogers, Willoughby; 1818 list age 72; served in N C line; drew pension in Blount Co; d June 23 1826.

Rogers, Wilson; 1840 Census age 82; drew pension in Lawrence Co; lived with Jacob Blyche, Sen.

Roland, Fendal; 1832 list age 74; also 1840 Census; served in N C mil; drew pension in Robertson Co.

Roland, James; 1832 list age 80; also 1840 Census; served in N C mil; drew pension in McNairy Co.

Roper, Drury; 1832 list age 70; served in Va mil; drew pension in Jefferson Co.

Ross, George; 1832 list age 74; also 1840 Census; served in S C mil; drew pension in Hardin Co.

Ross, John; 1832 list age 76; also 1840 Census; drew pension in Giles Co; in 1840 he lived with George B Ross.

Ross, John; 1840 Census age 88; drew pension in Stewart Co.

Ross, John; 1832 list age 77; served in N C mil; drew pension in Giles Co.

Ross, Robert; 1818 list age 78; served in Pa line; drew pension in Campbell Co.

Ross, Robinson; 1840 Census age 78; drew pension in Williamson Co.

Ross, Robinson; 1818 list age 75; served in Pa troops; drew pension in Maury Co.

Ross, Thomas M; drew pension in Nashville Agency.

Rosson, Archilaus; 1832 list age 84; served in Va mil; drew pension in Robertson Co.

Roulstone, Michael; drew pension in Knoxville Agency.

Rowe, Benjamin; 1832 list age 76; also 1840 Census; served in S C mil; drew pension in Lincoln Co.

Rowland, alias Rowlin, Thomas; served in 39th inf; lived in Knox Co; d in service Oct 19 1814; his heir was George Rowlin; (1812).

Rudd, Burlingham; 1832 list age 73; served in N C line; drew pension in Sevier Co; Sept 4 1837.

Rushing, Philip; 1840 Census age 78; drew pension in Perry Co; lived with Berrill Rushing.

Rushing, Richard; 1840 Census age 93; drew pension in Perry Co.

Russell, Buckner; 1832 list age 83; served in Va line; drew pension in Weakley Co.

Russell, George; 1818 list age 78; served in Va troops; drew pension in Smith Co; d Jan 2 1829.

Russell, James; 1828 list; drew pension in Tenn; county unknown; papers burned in War Office; d July 27 1819; (1812).

Russell, John; 1840 list age 55; served in 22nd reg't inf; drew pension in Jefferson Co; (1812).

Russell, Moses; 1832 list age 71; also 1840 Census; served in Va line; drew pension in Knox Co.

Russey, James, Sen; 1818 list age 79; served in Va line; drew pension in Franklin Co.

Rutherford, Absolom; 1832 list age 71; also 1840 Census; served in Va line; drew pension in Knox Co; d before 1841.

Rutherford, Julius; 1818 list age 75; served in Va line; drew pension in Anderson Co; d Aug 3 1831.

Rutherford, Thomas; 1818 list age 73; served in N C line; drew pension in Giles Co.

Rutherford, William; 1832 list age 85; served in Va mil; drew pension in Knox Co; d Dec 16 1833.

Rutland, Abenego; 1832 list age 76; served in N C line; drew pension in Williamson Co.

Rutledge, William; drew pension in Pulaski Agency.

Ryan, Harris; 1832 list age 70; also 1840 Census; served in Va line; drew pension in Rhea Co.

Sack, John, 1818 list age 80; served in Ga troops; drew pension in Rutherford Co.

Sadler, Benjamin; 1818 list age 68; served in Va troops; drew pension in Sumner Co; d Apr 3 1829.

Sadler, Benjamin; 1828 list; served in 1st reg't U S inf; drew pension in Sumner Co; transferred from Va; (1812).

Sage, John; 1818 list age 73; served in Va troops; drew pension in Maury Co; d Aug 13 1827.

Salts, John; drew pension in Jonesboro Agency.

Sample, Jesse; 1832 list age 70; served in S C line; drew pension in Rhea Co.

Sample, Samuel; 1832 list age 79; drew pension in Va line; drew pension in Knox Co.

Sanders, Cornelius; 1832 age 72; also 1840 Census; served in N C line; drew pension in Rutherford Co.

Sanders, James; 1832 list age 73; served in Va line; drew pension in Smith Co.

Sanders, John; 1832 list age 81; served in N C line; drew pension in Claiborne Co; d Apr 5 1833.

Sanders, Capt Richard; 1832 list age 77; served in N C line; drew pension in Wilson Co.

Sanders, Solomon; 1832 list age 94; served in N C line; drew pension in Franklin Co.

Sapp, Jesse; 1832 list age 71; served in Va line; drew pension in Warren Co.

Sarrett, Allen; 1832 list age 71; served in S C line; drew pension in Cocke Co.

Sarrett, John; 1832 list age 74; served in N C line; drew pension in Humphreys Co.

Sarrette, Samuel; 1818 list age 66; served in N C line; drew pension in Bedford Co.

Sartin, Eli; 1840 Census age 55; served in 7th U S rifles; drew pension in Jefferson Co; (1812).

Saunders, James; 1840 Census age 77; drew pension in Rutherford Co; lived with Mary Acuff.

Saunders, James; 1840 Census age 79; drew pension in DeKalb Co; lived with Joseph Saunders.

Savage, Levin; 1832 list age 84; served in N C line; drew pension in Jackson Co.

Sawyer, Eli; 1828 list; served in 1st reg't U S inf; drew pension in Summer Co; d Jan 24 1822; (1812).

Sawyer, Lewis; 1832 list age 87; served in N C mil; drew pension in Cocke Co.

Sawyers, James; 1832 list age 68; served in Va line; drew pension in Robertson Co.

Saylers, Michael; 1840 Census age 82; drew pension in Jackson Co; lived with Thomas Saylers.

Scally, William; 1818 list age 70; served in Va Continental line; drew pension in Davidson Co; d Jul 2 1823.

Schrimpler, Robert; 1832 list age 72; served in S C line; served in Monroe Co.

Schrimpler, Robert; 1832 list age 72; served in S C line; served in sion in Smith Co; his widow, Mary Schrivner, drew pension.

Scoby, John; 1840 Census age 66; drew pension in Dyer Co; (1812).

Scott, Arthur; 1832 list age 82; served in Va line; drew pension in Knox Co.

Scott, James; 1832 list age 79; served in N C line drew pension in Knox Co.

Scott, James; 1832 list age 71; served in N C line; drew pension in Wilson Co.

Scott, John; 1832 list age 80; also 1840 Census; drew pension in Carroll Co; in 1840 he lived with John McInturff.

Scott, John; 1828 list; served in N C line; drew pension in Wilson Co.

Scott, John; drew pension in Knoxville Agency; transferred to Jonesboro Agency; (Rev).

Scott, Reuben; 1818 list age 64; served in Va troops; drew pension in Rutherford Co; d before May 23 1824.

Scott, Thomas; 1832 list age 72; served in S C line; drew pension in Williamson Co.

Scott, Thomas, Sen; 1832 list age 79; served in N C line; drew pension in Fentress Co.

Scott, Lieut William; 1828 list; served in 24th reg't U S inf; drew pension in Knox Co; (1812).

Scudder, Mathias; 1828 list; served in Tenn mil; drew pension in Wilson Co; (1812).

Seamonds, Jonathan; 1832 list age 77; served in Va line; drew pension in Jefferson Co.

Seamore, Thomas; 1840 Census age 80; drew pension in Carroll Co; lived with William Seamore.

Secrest, John; 1832 list age 77; also 1840 Census; served in N C line; drew pension in Williamson Co.

Sellers, James; 1840 Census age 85; drew pension in Bradley Co.

Sellers, James; 1832 list age 75; served in N C line; drew pension in Grainger Co.

Semore, Thomas; 1832 list age 70; also 1840 Census; served in Va mil; drew pension in Carroll Co; (Seamore).

Senter, Tandy; 1840 Census age 82; drew pension in Roane Co.

Seratt, Allen; 1840 Census age 77; drew pension in Cocke Co.

Setton, William; 1818 list age 92; served in Va line; drew pension in Greene Co.

Sevier, Abraham; 1832 list age 72; also 1840 Census; served in N C troops; drew pension in Overton Co; lived with Abraham R Sevier.

Sevier, James; 1832 list age 70; also 1840 Census; drew pension in Washington Co.

Sevier, Naomi; 1840 Census age 97; drew pension in Greene Co where she lived with John Rector (a son-in-law); she was the widow of Valentine Sevier.

Sexton, John; 1840 list age 79; drew pension in Greene Co.

Sexton, Timothy; 1818 list age 79; served in N J line; drew pension in Campbell Co; his widow Esther Sexton 1840 Census age 79 drew pension in Morgan Co where she lived with her son Timothy Sexton.

Seypeart, Robert; 1818 list age 78; served in S C line; drew pension in Wayne Co.

Shackler, Philip; 1818 age 69; served in N C troops; drew pension in Sumner Co; d Oct 14 1821.

Shaffer, David; 1818 list age 73; served in N C troops; drew pension in Smith Co.

Shaffer, Frederick; 1832 list age 76; served in Va line; drew pension in Greene Co.

Shaffer, John; 1832 list age 78; served in Va line; drew pension in Sullivan Co.

Shannon, Archibald B; 1828 list; also 1840 Census age 48; served in Tenn vol; drew pension in 1828 in Wilson Co; drew pension in 1840 in Shelby Co; (1812).

Shannon, William; 1832 list age 77; served in Pa mil; drew pension in Grainger Co.

Sharp, Samuel; 1832 list age 77; served in Va line; drew pension in Knox Co.

Sharp, William; 1818 list; also 1840 Census age 79; served in Va line; drew pension in Greene Co.

Shaw, Benjamin; 1832 list age 72; served in N C; drew pension in Wayne Co where he lived with Hugh Liston.

Shaw, James; 1828 list; also 1840 Census age 69; served in reg't mounted gunmen; drew pension in 1828 in Bedford Co; drew pension in 1840 in Marshall Co; (1812).

Shaw, William; 1832 list age 73; served in Va line; drew pension in Davidson Co.

Shaw, William; 1832 list age 76; also 1840 Census; served in N C line; drew pension in Lincoln Co.

Shaw, Zachariah; 1832 list age 79; served in N C line; drew pension in Gibson Co.

Shelby, John; drew pension in Nashville Agency.

Shelton, George; 1832 list age 82; also 1840 Census; served in N C line; drew pension in Fentress Co; spelled Chilton in one list.

Shepherd, Samuel; 1832 list age 72; also 1840 Census; served in Va line; drew pension in Wilson Co.

Shepherd, Thomas; 1832 list age 79; served in Va mil; drew pension in Robertson Co.

Sherrill, George Davidson; 1832 list age 71; also 1840 Census; served in N C line; drew pension in 1832 in Franklin Co; drew pension in 1840 in Coffee Co.

Shields, John; 1832 list age 85; served in U S Navy from Pa; drew pension in Carter Co.

Shockley, Thomas; 1832 list age 78; also 1840 Census; served in Va line; drew pension in White Co.

Shortridge, Andrew; 1840 Census age 85; served in Va troops; drew pension in Fentress Co; his widow, Nancy Shortridge, drew pension.

Shropshire, William; 1818 list age 74; served in N C troops; drew pension in White Co.

Shumate, Lieut W J; 1828 list; served in Williamson's mil; drew pension in Williamson Co; (1812).

Shurman, Charles, see Charles Thurman.

Sikes, Thomas A; 1818 list age 74; served in Va line; drew pension in Rutherford Co.

Silver, Aaron; 1832 list age 76; served in Va mil; drew pension in Hawkins Co.

Simonds, Nevitt; 1832 list age 83; served in N C line; drew pension in Rutherford Co.

Simmonds, James, Sen; 1840 Census age 81; drew pension in Hawkins Co.

Simons, James; 1818 list age 76; served in Va line; drew pension in Hawkins Co; probably same as above James Simmonds.

Simmons, James; 1840 Census age 49; drew pension in Washington Co; (1812).

Simmons, Jesse; 1832 list age 73; served in S C line; drew pension in Robertson Co.

Simmons, Joseph; 1832 list age 79; served in Va line; drew pension in Greene Co.

Simmons, Polly, widow; 1840 Census age 74; drew pension in Henry Co where she lived with James P Simmons.

Simms, James; see James Symms.

Simms, John; 1832 list age 90; drew pension in Monroe Co; lived with John Gentry.

Simpson, Lockey; 1828 list; served in 7th U S inf; drew pension in Tenn; county unknown; papers destroyed when the War Office was burned; (1812).

Sims, John; 1832 list age 83; served in N C line; drew pension in Blount Co.

Sims, Micajah; 1818 list age 74; served in Va troops; drew pension in Smith Co; d Jan 20, 1824; his widow Elizabeth Sims, also drew pension.

Singleton, Robert; 1818 list age 80; served in N C troops; drew pension in Montgomery Co; d Jan 31 1821.

Sisk, Bartlett; 1832 list age 75; served in N C line; drew pension in Cocke Co.

Sisk, William; 1832 list age 72; also 1840 Census; served in N C line; drew pension in Hawkins Co.

Skelton, William; 1832 list age 72; also 1840 Census; served in N C line; drew pension in Hawkins Co.

Skipper, Nathan; 1818 list age 78; served in N C troops; drew pension in Maury Co.

Slape, Thomas; 1818 list age 79; served in Va line; drew pension in Campbell Co; d Mar 26 1821.

Slaton, James; 1832 list age 75; served Va line; drew pension in Bedford Co.

Slaughter, Bernard; 1828 list; served in 1st reg't U. S. rifles; drew pension in Williamson Co; (1812).

Slaughter, Jacob; 1818 list age 78; also 1840 Census; served in N C line; drew pension in Sullivan Co.

Slaughter, William; 1832 list age 78; also 1840 Census; served in Va line; drew pension in Washington Co; lived with David Lawson.

Sleeker, George; 1828 list; served in 2nd reg't; Tenn mil; drew pension in Williamson Co; (1812).

Sloane, Arthur; 1828 list; served in McCormack's company U S art; drew pension in Carter Co; (1812).

Sloane, John; 1832 list age 75; also 1840 Census; served in N C mil; drew pension in Sumner Co.

Smallwood, Elisha; 1828 list; served in 24th reg't U S inf; drew pension in Sullivan Co; (1812).

Smallwood, William; served in Rev; drew pension in Sevier Co.

Smartt, Alexander; served in rifle reg't; lived in Cocke Co; d in service Dec 1813; his heirs were: Nancy, Sally, Joseph and Samuel Smartt; (1812).

Smith, Charles; 1840 Census age 88; served in Washington Cav; drew pension in Wilson Co where he lived with Archibald Ray.

Smith, Cobb; 1818 list age 74; served in N C line; drew pension in Sullivan Co.

Smith, Elijah; 1832 list age 79; served in N C line; drew pension in Rutherford Co.

Smith, Elijah; 1818 list age 73; served in Va line; drew pension in Davidson Co.

Smith, Edward; 1832 list age 79; 1840 Census; served in Va line; drew pension in Knox Co.

Smith, Garnett; 1832 list age 71; also 1840 Census; served in Va line; drew pension in Knox Co; lived with Bolin Smith.

Smith, George; 1832 list age 73; also 1840 Census; served in N C line; drew pension in Davidson Co.

Smith, George, Sen; 1832 list age 71; served in N C line; drew pension in Bedford Co.

Smith, Henry; 1832 list age 81; served in Va mil; drew pension in McMinn Co.

Smith, James; 1828 list; drew pension in Maury Co; his pension commenced 1796; papers were destroyed when the War Office was burned; he died before 1832.

Smith, Joel; 1832 list age 73; served in Va line; drew pension in White Co.

Smith, John; 1832 list age 78; served in Va line; drew pension in Hawkins Co; his widow, Elizabeth Smith, 1840 Census age 79, lived with Joseph Mooney.

Smith, John 1st; 1832 list age 74; served in N C line; drew pension in Franklin Co.

Smith, John 2nd; 1832 list age 71; served in N C line; drew pension in Henry Co.

Smith, Joshua; 1818 list age 81; served in Va troops; drew pension in Rutherford Co.

Smith, Laton; 1832 list age 78; also 1840 Census; served in Va line; drew pension in 1832 in Bledsoe Co; drew pension in 1840 in Marion Co.

Smith, Nathaniel; 1828 list; served in 39th reg't U S inf; drew pension in Wilson Co; (1812).

Smith, Obadiah; 1832 list age 71; served in Va mil; drew pension in Jefferson Co.

Smith, Philip; 1832 list age 77; served in N C line; drew pension in Monroe Co; d 1839.

Smith, Ransome; 1832 list age 73; also 1840 Census; served in N C mil; drew pension in Marion Co.

Smith, Ralph; 1832 list age 76; also 1840 Census; served in S C line; drew pension in Lincoln Co.

Smith, Lieut Robert; 1818 list age 84; served in N C line; drew pension in Hawkins Co.

Smith, Samuel; 1818 list age 71; served in N C troops; drew pension in Hickman Co.

Smith, Sherrod; 1840 Census age 79; drew pension in Williamson Co.

Smith, Skiller; 1832 list age 72; served in Va mil; drew pension in Sumner Co.

Smith, W C; 1832 list age 72; also 1840 Census; served in N C line; drew pension in Lincoln Co; lived with Larkin Smith.

Smith, William; 1832 list age 72; served in Va line; drew pension in Lincoln Co.

Smith, William; 1828 list; served in West Tenn mil; drew pension in Lincoln Co; (1812).

Smith, William; 1828 list; served in 2nd reg't Tenn mil; drew pension in Bedford Co; (1812).

Smith, William; 1832 list age 71; served in Va line; drew pension in Robertson Co.

Smith, William; 1832 list age 89; served in Pa line; drew pension in Washington Co.

Smith, William; 1832 list age 89; served in N C mil; drew pension in Jefferson Co.

Smith, Willis; see Willis, Smith.

Smith, Zachariah; 1832 list age 77; also 1840 Census; served in N C line; drew pension in Williamson Co; lived with Charles S McCall.

Smith, Zebulon; 1832 list age 75; served in Va mil; drew pension in Sullivan Co.

Smithpeter, John M; 1832 list age 81; served in Va line; drew pension in Washington Co.

Snodgrass, William; 1832 list age 74; also 1840 Census; served in Va line; drew pension in Sullivan Co.

Snow, Ebenezer; 1832 list age 76; served in Pa line; drew pension in Roane Co.

Sowell, John; 1832 list age 73; also 1840 Census; served in Va line; drew pension in Hawkins Co; in 1840 he lived with William Ritter.

Sparks, Mathew; 1832 list age 76; also 1840 Census; served in N C line; drew pension in Carroll Co; in 1840 he lived with Isaac Sparks, Sen.

Spears, Joseph; 1818 list age 74; also 1840 Census; served in N C troops; drew pension in Lawrence Co.

Spears, Samuel; 1818 list age 73; served in N C line; drew pension in Hawkins Co.

Spencer, Moses; 1818 list age 91; served in Va troops; drew pension in Maury Co; d Mar 21 1826.

Spradling, James; 1818 list age 84; served in Va line; drew pension in Claiborne Co.

Spradling, John; 1832 list age 86; served in N C line; drew pension in Warren Co.

Spragen, Thomas; 1818 list age 78; served in Va line; drew pension in Monroe Co.

Stanfield, James; 1832 list age 81; served in N C line; drew pension in McMinn Co.

Stansbury, Luke; 1818 list age 76; also 1840 Census; served in N C line; drew pension in Knox Co.

Standifer, Benjamin; 1832 list age 70; served in N C mil; drew pension in Bledsoe Co.

Standley, Sims; 1832 list age 71 served in N C mil; drew pension in Shelby Co.

Staples, John; 1818 list age 77; served in Va line; drew pension in Morgan Co; his widow, Betsy Staples, drew pension, 1840 Census age 76; lived with B Staples.

Stapleton, William; 1832 list age 72; served in N C line; drew pension in Hawkins Co.

Starrett, Benjamin; 1840 Census age 76; served in Lee's Legion; drew pension in Fayette Co.

Steed, Thomas; 1832 list age 75; served in Va mil; drew pension in McMinn Co.

Steel, Samuel; 1832 list age 74; also 1840 Census; served in Va mil; drew pension in Monroe Co.

Steele, Hanna Morrison Steele, widow of George Steele of Monroe Co, applied for pension in Jefferson Co Aug 6 1835.

Steele, Samuel; 1832 list age 72; served in N C mil; drew pension in Maury Co.

Stephens, Henry; 1840 Census age 66 served in Williamson's Tenn mil; drew pension in Monroe Co; lived with Nathaniel Watson; (1812).

Stephens, Meshack; 1832 list age 78; served in Va State line; drew pension in Marion Co.

Stephens, Robert; 1832 list age 77; served in Va line; drew pension in Lincoln Co.

Stephenson, John; 1832 list also 1840 Census age 87; served in N C line; drew pension in Rutherford Co; lived with Enos McNight.

Stephenson, John; 1840 Census age 89; drew pension in Cannon Co; lived with Abner Alexander.

Steptoe, Simon S; 1832 list age 73; also 1840 Census; served in N C line; drew pension in Humphreys Co; lived with Hilary Caps.

Sterling, Robert; 1832 list age 74; served in Va mil; drew pension in Blount Co.

Stewart, Barney; 1832 list age 72; served in N C line; drew pension in Sumner Co.

Stewart, John; 1840 Census age 83; drew pension in McNairy Co where he lived with Jane Edwards.

Stewart, Simeon; served in 1st reg't rifles; lived in Warren Co; d in service Sept 17 1814; his heirs were: Alexander, Isaac, James and Rachel; (1812).

Stewart, Robert; 1818 list age 87; served in Md troops; drew pension in Williamson Co.

Stewart, William; 1818 list age 79; served in Va troops; drew pension in Madison Co.

Stewart, William; 1818 list age 79; served in Md troops; drew pension in White Co; d June 25 1829.

Stokeley, Thomas; 1828 list; served in Gray's Rifle reg't; drew pension in Haywood Co; (1812).

Stone, Conway, 1832 list age 73; served in N C line; drew pension in Monroe Co; d Nov 19 1834.

Stone, Ezekial; 1832 list age 78; also 1840 Census; served in N C state troops; drew pension in Marion Co; lived with Richard W Stone.

Stone, John; 1840 Census age 76; drew pension in Rutherford Co.

Stone, John; 1818 list age 73; served in Pa troops; drew pension in Lawrence Co.

Stone, Solomon; 1832 list age 81; served in N C line; drew pension in Marion Co.

Stone, Stephen; 1832 list age 83; served in Va line; drew pension in Sumner Co.

Stonecipher, Joseph; 1832 list age 78; also 1840 Census; served in N C line; drew pension in Morgan Co.

Stonecipher, Mark; drew pension in Knoxville Agency; (Rev).

Stoval, Bartholomew; 1832 list age 74; also 1840 Census; served in Va line; drew pension in Sumner Co.

Strain, John; 1832 list age 74; served in N C mil; drew pension in Washington Co.

Street, Isaac; 1832 list age 71; also 1840 Census; drew pension in Franklin Co.

Stricklin, Frederick; 1818 list age 83; served in N C troops; drew pension in Lawrence Co; d Nov 1 1825.

Strome, Richard; 1832 list age 72; served in N C line; drew pension in Hardin Co; the name is spelled Strome in 1840 Census and Strown in 1832 list.

Strong, Christopher; 1832 list age 74; also 1840 Census; served in S C line drew pension in Dickson Co.

Stuckeberry, Jacob; 1818 list age 78; served in Va line; drew pension in Campbell Co.

Sturman, William; 1818 list age 77; served in Va troops; drew pension in Warren Co; d Jan 30 1832.

Swain, Charles; drew pension in Jonesboro Agency.

Suddoth, Benjamin; 1832 list age 74; served in S C line; drew pension in Roane Co.

Sullivan, George; 1832 list age 73; served in Va line; drew pension in White Co.

Sumpter, Thomas; 1832 list age 72; 1840 Census; served in N C line; drew pension in Knox Co.

Sutherland, Daniel; 1832 list age 80; served in N C line; drew pension in Bledsoe Co.

Sutherland, John; 1818 list age 81; served in N C troops; drew pension in Smith Co; d May 26 1824.

Suttle, Edward; 1832 list age 69; served in Va line; drew pension in Smith Co.

Sutton, John; 1832 list age 83; also 1840 Census; served in S C mil; drew pension in 1832 in Rhea Co; drew pension in 1840 in Meigs Co; lived with Thomas P. Davis.

Swadley, Mark; 1832 list age 74; served in Va line; drew pension in Monroe Co.

Swadley, Marcus, no doubt the same as above; 1840 Census age 80; drew pension in Knox Co; lived with Ann Defriese.

Swallow, Andrew; 1832 list age 74; also 1840 Census; drew pension in Overton Co.

Swatzel, Philip; 1832 list age 76; served in Pa line; drew pension in Greene Co.

Sweet, Allen; 1818 list age 69; also 1840 Census; drew pension in Lincoln Co; transferred from Wake Co N C; drew pension in 1840 in McNairy Co; name is spelled Sweet in 1818 list and Sweat in 1840 Census.

Swindle, John; 1832 list age 74; served in N C line; drew pension in Humphreys Co.

Sykes, James; 1832 list age 73; served in N C line; drew pension in Lincoln Co.

Sykes, Thomas A; see Thomas A Sikes.

Symms, also Simms, James; 1832 list age 83; also 1840 Census; served in Va mil; drew pension in Blount Co; lived with John Symms.

Sypert, William L; 1840 Census age 45; served in Williamson's mil; drew pension in Wilson Co; (1812).

Tacke, John; 1840 Census age 86; drew pension in Bedford Co.

Tally, John; 1828 list; served in Washington Cav; drew pension in Perry Co.

Tankersly, John; 1832 list age 72; served in Navy on the U S Ship Tartar.

Tankersly, William; served in 3rd reg inf; lived in Blount Co; d in service Oct 1814; his heirs were: John, Washington and Lucinda Tankersly; (1812).

Tanner, John; 1840 Census age 81; drew pension in Grainger Co.

Tarver, Samuel; 1840 Census age 80; drew pension in Knox Co.

Tate, David; 1832 list age 75; served in Va mil; drew pension in Grainger Co.

Tate, John; 1818 list age 89; served in N J troops; drew pension in Smith Co.

Tatum, Lieut James; 1818 list age 64; served in N C line; drew pension in Davidson Co; d Sept 10 1821.

Tatum, Nathaniel; 1832 list age 75; 1840 Census age 79; drew pension in Giles Co.

Tatorn, William; 1840 Census age 80; drew pension in Dickson Co.

Taylor, Andrew; 1832 list age 69; also 1840 Census; served in N C line; drew pension in Carter Co.

Taylor, Charles; 1832 list age 80; served in S C line; drew pension in Bedford Co.

Taylor, Capt Christopher; served in N C mil; drew pension in Washington Co; d Sept 10 1833.

Taylor, Daniel; 1832 list age 72; served in Va line; drew pension in Grainger Co.

Taylor, Lieut and Ensign Isaac; 1832 list age 78; served in N C line; drew pension in Carter Co.

Taylor, James; 1832 list age 74; also 1840 Census; served in N C line; drew pension in Blount Co; lived with Joshua Taylor.

Taylor, James; 1828 list; served Gaskin's reg't; drew pension in Franklin Co; transferred from Va; his pension dated from 1785; (Rev).

Taylor, Joseph, Sen; 1840 Census age 78; drew pension in Overton Co.

Taylor, LeRoy; 1832 list age 76; served in N C mil; drew pension in Washington Co.

Taylor, Lewis; 1832 list age 79; served in N C line; drew pension Franklin Co.

Taylor, Samuel; 1818 list age 79; also 1840 Census; served in Va line; drew pension in Sullivan Co; lived with Edward Taylor.

Taylor, Thomas; 1818 list age 79; served in Va troops; drew pension in Sumner Co.

Tays, Samuel; 1832 list age 79; also 1840 Census; served in N C mil; drew pension in Overton Co.

Teague, William; 1832 list age 73; also 1840 Census; served in S C line; drew pension in Wilson Co; lived with John Pemberton.

Tedford, Robert; 1832 list age 74; also 1840 Census; served in Va line; drew pension in Blount Co; lived with Robert A Tedford.

Telford, Hugh; 1832 list age 69; served in N C line; drew pension in Wilson Co.

Terry, Thomas; 1832 list age 78; served in N C line; drew pension in Smith Co.

Tench, John; 1832 list age 76; served in Va line; drew pension in Rutherford Co.

Thacker, Ambrose 1832 list age 76; served in N C line; drew pension in Fentress Co.

Thacker, Benjamin; 1832 list age 73; served in Va line; drew pension in Roane Co.

Thacker, William; 1818 list age 94; served in Va line; drew pension in Washington Co.

Thomas, Henry; 1832 list age 76; served in N C mil; drew pension in Dyer Co.

Thomas, Jacob; 1818 list age 75; served in Va line; drew pension in Knox Co; d Feb 28 1831.

Thomas, James; 1832 list age 77; served in N C line; drew pension in Gibson Co.

Thomas, John; 1832 list; drew pension in Lincoln Co.

Thomas, John; 1818 list age 59; served in Md troops; drew pension in Wilson Co.

Thomas, John; 1832 list age 73; served in Va line; drew pension in Bledsoe Co.

Thomas, Joseph; 1832 list age 71; served in Pa line; drew pension in Lawrence Co.

Thomas, Nottley; 1832 list age 81; also 1840 Census; served in S C mil; drew pension in Hawkins Co.

Thomas, Reuben; 1828 list; served in 1st reg't rifles; drew pension in Jefferson Co.

Thomas, Robert; 1832 list age 75; served in N C line; drew pension in Davidson Co.

Thomas, Stephen; 1828 list; served in Armstrong's reg't; drew pension in Montgomery Co; transferred from N C; d May 10 1825; pension commenced in 1798.

Thomas, William; 1832 list age 80; served in N C line; drew pension in Weakley Co.

Thomas, William; 1832; list served in S C line; drew pension in Dyer Co; d Apr 1 1833.

Thomason, George; 1818 list age 78; served in Mass troops; drew pension in Smith Co; d May 4 1833.

Thompson, Burwell; 1832 list age 74; served in S C line; drew pension in Franklin Co.

Thompson, Charles; 1832 list age 74; served in Va line; drew pension in Dickson Co; his widow Mary Thompson drew pension in 1840 age 71.

Thompson, Hudson; 1832 list age 72; also 1840 Census; served in N C mil; drew pension in Sumner Co.

Thompson, John; drew pension in Knoxville Agency.

Thompson, Samuel; 1832 list age 80; served in Va line; drew pension in Blount Co.

Thompson, Stephen; 1832 list age 70; served in S C line; drew pension in Marion Co.

Thompson, Thomas; 1832 list age 74; served in N C line; drew pension in McMinn Co.

Thompson, Thomas; 1832 list age 75; served in N C line; drew pension in Davidson Co.

Thompson, Capt William; 1832 list age 81; served in N C line; drew pension in Franklin Co.

Thornburgh, John; 1840 Census age 61; served in 24th reg't rifles; drew pension in Washington Co; (1812).

Thornton, Pressley; 1832 list age 76; served in Va line; drew pension in Weakley Co; lived with William Jones.

Thorpe, John; 1840 Census age 63; served in 5th reg't U S inf; drew pension in Hardin Co; (1812).

Thurman, Charles; 1832 list age 74; also 1840 Census; served in S C mil; drew pension in Bledsoe Co; name is spelled Shurman on one list but that is an error.

Thurman, Nancy, widow of John Thurman; applied for pension in Blount Co in 1845.

Thurman, Philip; 1832 list age 76; also 1840 Census; served in S C mil; drew pension in Bledsoe Co; name is spelled Shurman on one list but that is an error.

Thurman, William; 1832 list age 73; also 1840 Census; served in Va line; drew pension in Hawkins Co; lived with Benjamin Thurman.

Tilton, Philip; 1828 list; served in 1st reg't rifles; drew pension in Knox Co; (1812).

Tinner, James; 1840 Census age 81; drew pension in Giles Co.

Tinsley, Cornelius; 1832 list age 85; served in N C line; drew pension in Sumner Co.

Tinsley, John; 1832 list age 87; served in Va line; drew pension in Sumner Co.

Tipper, William; 1818 list age 65; served in N C line; drew pension in Bedford Co; d Feb 4 1834.

Tippitt, Erastus; 1818 list age 70; served in N C troops; drew pension in Lawrence Co.

Tipton, Jonathan; 1832 list age 84; served in N C line; drew pension in Overton Co; d Jan 18 1833.

Tipton, Jonathan; age 81; also 1840 Census; served in Md line; drew pension in Wilson Co; lived with James Tipton.

Tipton, William; 1832 list age 73; also 1840 Census; served in Va line; drew pension in 1832 in Knox Co; drew pension in 1840 in Blount Co.

Titlow (Tilton in 1828 list), Philip; 1840 Census age 57; drew pension in Knox Co; (1812).

Todd, Benjamin; 1832 list; also 1840 Census age 78; served in N C mil; drew pension in Rutherford Co.

Toff (or Taff), George; 1832 list age 70; served in Va line; drew pension in Jefferson Co.

Tolly, John; 1840 Census age 78; drew pension in Perry Co.

Toney, William; 1828 list; served in 5th U S inf; drew pension in Carter Co; transferred from Va; (1812).

Towaug, Henry; 1818 list age 69; served in Armand's Legion; drew pension in Greene Co.

Towler, Benjamin; 1832 list age 82; served in Va line; drew pension in Rutherford Co.

Towner, John; 1832 list age 75; served in N C line; drew pension in Hawkins Co.

Towns, Thomas; 1840 Census age 89; drew pension in Polk Co where he lived with John Towns.

Townsend, George; 1832 list age 79; served in N C line; drew pension in Claiborne Co.

Townsend, John; 1828 list; served in Washington Cav; drew pension in Carroll Co; (1812).

Townsend, Joshua; 1832 list age 72; served in Va line; drew pension in Franklin Co.

Trail, James; 1832 list age 77; served in Va line; drew pension in Greene Co.

Trainum, William; 1832 list age 90; served in N C mil; drew pension in Sumner Co.

Trammell, Dennis; 1840 Census; drew pension in Campbell Co where he lived with David Trammell.

Travis, Thomas; 1832 list age 75; served in Pa line; drew pension in Fentress Co.

Treace, Michael; 1832 list age 75; also 1840 Census; served in Pa line; drew pension in 1832 in Grainger Co; drew pension in 1840 in Jefferson Co.

Treadway, Robert; 1832 list age 73; served in N C line; drew pension in Sullivan Co.

Trent, Alexander; 1840 Census age 81; drew pension in Hawkins Co.

Tribbett, Robert; 1840 Census age 57; drew pension in Sullivan Co; (1812).

Trice, James; 1832 list age 72; served in Va line; drew pension in Blount Co.

Trotter, William; 1832 list age 71; also 1840 Census; served in Va line; drew pension in Sevier Co.

Trout, Jacob; 1840 Census age 105; drew pension in Gibson Co; lived with Joseph Trout.

Trowell, James; 1832 list age 88; also 1840 Census; served in N C line; drew pension in Anderson Co.

Troxall, Jacob; 1832 list age 75; served in Va line; drew pension in Marion Co.

True, Martin; 1818 list age 74; also 1840 Census; served in Va troops; drew pension in 1832 in Williamson Co; drew pension in 1840 in Maury Co.

Tucker, David; 1832 list age 80; served in N C line; drew pension in Bedford Co.

Tucker, John; 1840 Census age 87; drew pension in Hickman Co.

Tucker, Sylvanus; 1840 Census age 84; drew pension in Rutherford Co; lived with David Tucker.

Tucker, Thomas; 1832 list age 83; served in Md line; drew pension in Warren Co.

Tulbock, John D; 1828 list; served in 2nd Tenn mil; drew pension in Blount Co; d Feb 18 1832.

Tulloch, Magnus; 1832 list age 70; served in S C line as a fifer; drew pension in Blount Co.

Turbeyfield, William; 1832 list age 84: served in N C line; drew pension in Robertson Co.

Turner, Charles; 1840 list age 75; drew pension in Fayette Co; lived with Colin Turner.

Turner, James; 1832 list age 78; served in N C line; drew pension in Williamson Co.

Turner, John T; 1828 list; served in 4th reg't Md line; drew pension in Stewart Co; d April 27 1831; widow was Mary Turner.

Turnley, George; 1840 Census age 78; served in Va troops in Rev; served in Tenn mil in War of 1812; drew pension in Jefferson Co.

Turnley, John; 1818 list age 79; served in Va troops; drew pension in Warren Co; d Dec 7 1832.

Tyner, Dempsey; 1832 list age 79; served in S C line; drew pension in Hamilton Co.

Tyree, William; 1832 list age 81; served in Va line; drew pension in Smith Co; his widow Sarah Tyree, drew pension.

Usselton, George; 1832 list age 73; served in Md line; drew pension in Rutherford Co.

Vales, Sames; 1840 Census age 82; drew pension in Hardeman Co where he lived with Samuel Vales.

Vandeford, James; 1832 list age 73; served in N C line; drew pension in Hickman Co.

Vance, Samuel; 1832 list age 80; served in Va line; drew pension in Greene Co.

Vandegriff, Jacob; 1832 list age 74; served in Va mil; drew pension in Grainger Co.

Varner, Henry; 1832 list age 93; served in N C line; drew pension in Greene Co.

Vaughn, Abraham; 1832 list age 63; served in N C line; drew pension in Wilson Co.

Vernon, Col Richard; 1832 list age 76; also 1840 Census; served in N C mil; drew pension in Williamson Co; lived with Leonard Vernon.

Vernon, Thomas; 1840 Census age 88; drew pension in Monroe Co.

Vick, John; 1832 list age 77; also 1840 Census; served in N C mil; drew pension in Montgomery Co.

Vick, Joseph; 1840 Census age 78; drew pension in Davidson Co.

Vickery, Luke; 1832 list age 83; drew pension in Marion Co.

Vickers, John R; 1840 Census age 91; drew pension in Lincon Co.

Voss, Vincent; 1840 Census age 84; drew pension in Tipton Co where he lived with E O Chambers.

Waddle, David; 1828 list; served in 1st reg't U S rifles; drew pension in Sevier Co.

Waddle, Jacob; served in 24th reg't inf; lived in Sullivan Co; captured at Fort Niagra; his heirs were: Polly, Parmelia, Henry, Jacob and Harmon Waddle; (1812).

Waddle, Martin; 1832 list age 71; also 1840 Census; served in N C line; drew pension in Greene Co.

Wadkins, Samuel; 1840 Census age 80; drew pension in Benton Co.

Wagnor (Waggoner), Lieut John P; 1818 list; served in Ga troops; drew pension in Sumner Co; transferred from Barren Co Ky; d Aug 22 1828.

Wakefield, Abel; 1832 list age 70; served in Va line; drew pension in Lawrence Co.

Wakefield, Henry; 1832 list age 83; also 1840 Census; served in N C line; drew pension in Smith Co.

Wakefield, Thomas; 1832 list age 72; also 1840 Census; served in S C line; drew pension in Franklin Co.

Walker, Edward; 1832 list age 77; served in N C line; drew pension in Claiborne Co.

Walker, George; 1832 list age 89; served in N C mil; drew pension in Bledsoe Co.

Walker, Isaac; 1832 list age 76; also 1840 Census; served in N C line; drew pension in Dickson Co.

Walker, James; 1828 list; served in Tenn vol; drew pension in Henry Co; (1812).

Walker, John; 1818 list age 57; served in S C line; drew pension in Davidson Co; d Jul 7 1829.

Walker, John; 1832 list age 84; served in Pa line; drew pension in Blount Co; his widow Mary Walker filed claim in 1844.

Walker, John; 1818 list age 79; served in Va line; drew pension in Roane Co; d Jul 7 1829.

Walker, Richard; 1818 list age 79; served in Va line; drew pension in Bedford Co.

Walker, Robert; 1832 list age 77; served in Md line; drew pension in Bedford Co.

Walker, Capt Samuel; 1818 list age 80; served in Va line; drew pension in Roane Co; d Jul 8 1830.

Walker, Samuel; 1840 Census age 80; drew pension in Roane Co where he lived with William Parker.

Walker, Samuel; 1832 list age 80; served in N C mil; drew pension in Smith Co.

Walker, William; 1832 list age 74; served in N C line; drew pension in Hardin Co.

Walker, William W; 1840 Census age 25; drew pension in Robertson Co; (1812).

Wallace, Edward; 1832 list age 79; served in Va mil; drew pension in Carter Co.

Wallace, Samuel; 1832 list age 74; served in N C line; drew pension in Jackson Co.

Walling, John; 1832 list age 84; served in Va line; drew pension in McMinn Co.

Walling, William; 1832 list age 75; served in N C mil; drew pension in Hawkins Co.

Wallis, Benjamin; 1832 list age 77; served in N C line; drew pension in Hawkins Co.

Wallis, Mathew; 1832 list age 71; served in N C line; drew pension in Bedford Co.

Washburn, Thomas; 1828 list; served in 1st reg't rifles; drew pension in Weakley Co; transferred from Ind.

Walton, Elizabeth Emmett, widow of Capt William Walton; drew pension in Sullivan Co.

Walton, Martin; 1832 list age 72; also 1840 Census; served in Va line; drew pension in Robertson Co.

Warren, Drury; 1832 list age 78; served in Va line; drew pension in Robertson Co.

Warren, Elijah; 1840 Census age 87; drew pension in Hardeman Co; lived with William Warren.

Warren, John; 1832 list age 75; served in Va line; drew pension in Rutherford Co.

Warren, John; 1832 list age 69; served in N C line; drew pension in Smith Co.

Washington, Susan, widow of William I Washington; drew pension in Nashville Agency.

Waters, Benjamin C; 1840 Census age 92; drew pension in Dickson Co.

Waters, James; Sen; 1818 list age 86; also 1840 Census; served in Va troops; drew pension in Lawrence Co.

Watkins, John; 1840 Census age 83; drew pension in Giles Co.

Watkins, Samuel; 1832 list age 74; served in N C line; drew pension in Humphreys Co.

Watkins, Spencer; 1832 list age 84; also 1840 Census; served in Va line; drew pension in Jefferson Co.

Watkins, William, 1832 list age 79; also 1840 Census; drew pension in 1832 in Williamson Co; drew pension in 1840 in Davidson Co; lived with William E Watkins.

Watson, Nathaniel; 1832 list age 90; also 1840 Census; served in S C line; drew pension in Monroe Co; lived with John Harris.

Watson, Samuel; 1840 Census age 79; drew pension in Giles Co; lived with Richard Suttle.

Watts, George; 1832 list age 72; served in S C line; drew pension in Jackson Co.

Wear, John; 1832 list age 93; served in N C line; drew pension in Sevier Co.

Weaver, John; 1832 list age 72; also 1840 Census; served in N C line; drew pension in White Co.

Weaver, Samuel; 1832 list age 75; also 1840 Census; served in N C line; drew pension in White Co; lived with Reuben Briles.

Weaver, Shadrach; 1832 list age 68; also 1840 Census; served in N C line; drew pension in 1832 in Maury Co; drew pension in 1840 in Marshall Co.

Webb, Benjamin; 1832 list age 79; served in Pa line; drew pension in Sullivan Co.

Webb, Jesse; 1832 list age 68; also 1840; served in N C line; drew pension in Jefferson Co.

Webb, Jesse; 1840 Census age 63; served in Tenn mil; drew pension in Claiborne Co; (1812).

Webb, John; 1832 list age 82; served in N C line; drew pension in Lincoln Co.

Webb, John; 1828 list; served in 44th reg't U S inf; drew pension in Lincoln Co; (1812).

Weeks, John; 1832 list age 80; served in N C line; drew pension in Perry Co.

Weeks, Joseph; 1832 list age 74; served in N C mil; drew pension in Montgomery Co.

Wees, Peter; 1832 list age 71; served in Va line; drew pension in Roane Co.

Weese, Michael; 1818 list age 82; served in Va line; drew pension in Greene Co; d Apr 20 1829.

Weety, John; 1818 list age 90; served in Md line; drew pension in Greene Co.

Weir, Margaret, widow of James Weir; filed claim in Blount Co in 1845.

Welch, John; 1832 list age 77; served in Va mil; drew pension in Weakley Co.

Welch, Robert; served in Rev; drew pension in Grainger Co.

Welch, Thomas; 1832 list age 85; also 1840 Census; served in N C line; drew pension in White Co.

Wells, Andrew; 1832 list age 79; served in N C line; drew pension in Sevier Co; d Feb 16 1834.

Wells, Jesse; 1832 list age 84; also 1840 Census; served in N C line; drew pension in Knox Co; lived with Michael Davis.

Wells, William; 1832 list age 79; served in Va line; drew pension in Giles Co; d Aug 20 1833.

Wells, Zachariah; 1818 list age 89; served in Va line; drew pension in Sullivan Co.

Welsh, Robert; 1832 list age 74; served in Va line; drew pension in Grainger Co.

Welty, John; 1818 list age 90; served in Md line; drew pension in Greene Co.

West, George; 1832 list age 84; served in N C line; drew pension in Rutherford Co.

West, Levi; 1818 list age 73; served in N Y line; drew pension in Rutherford Co; d Oct 8 1830.

West, William; 1832 list age 81; served in N C line; drew pension in Robertson Co.

Westmoreland, Jesse; 1832 list age 80; drew pension in Fentress Co.

Wheatley, Alexander; 1832 list age 76; served in N C mil; drew pension in Weakley Co.

Wheeler, Joseph; drew pension in Nashville Agency.

Wheeler, Samuel; 1828 list; served in 39th reg't U S inf; drew pension in McMinn Co; (1812).

Whelan, Richard; 1818 list age 79; served in Md line; drew pension in Anderson Co.

Whitaker, Richard; 1832 list age 72; served in N C mil; drew pension in Lincoln Co.

White, Benjamin; 1818 list; served in N C troops; drew pension in Maury Co; d June 18 1832.

White, George; 1832 list age 78; served in N C line; drew pension in Giles Co.

White, Gordon; 1832 list age 72; served in Va line; drew pension in Blount Co.

White, Govan; 1832 list age 68; served in Va line; drew pension in Robertson Co; his widow, Ann White, 1840 Census age 81 also drew pension.

White, John, Sen; 1832 list age 77; also 1840 Census; served in Va line; drew pension in White Co.

White, Robert; 1832 list age 79; served in Va line; drew pension in White Co.

White, Samuel; 1832 list age 79; served in S C line; drew pension in Williamson Co.

White, Stephen; 1832 list age 76; also 1840 Census; served in N C line; drew pension in Rutherford Co.

White, Thomas; 1832 list age 75; served in N C line; drew pension in Wilson Co.

White, William; 1832 list age 78; served in N C line; drew pension in Blount Co.

White, William; 1832 list age 80; served in N C line; drew pension in Lincoln Co.

White, William; 1832 list age 82; served in N C line; drew pension in Anderson Co.

Whiteman, Patrick; 1832 list age 78; served in Pa line; drew pension in Sullivan Co.

Whiteside, William; 1832 list age 70; also 1840 Census; served in S C mil; drew pension in Carroll Co; in 1840 he lived with John Whiteside.

Whitfield, Willis; 1832 list age 79; served in N C line; drew pension in Rutherford Co.

Whitman, John; 1832 list age 84; served in Va line; drew pension in Campbell Co.

Wiette, Edmund; 1832 list age 78; served in Va line; drew pension in Anderson Co.

Wiggins, William; 1832 list age 74; served in N C line; drew pension in Montgomery Co.

Willburn, Joshua; 1832 list age 76; served in N C line; drew pension in Carroll Co.

Wiley, Alexander; see Alexander Wyley.

Wiley, Lieut William; 1832 list age 84; also 1840 Census; served in N C mil; drew pension in Dickson Co; lived with William Willie.

Wilkerson, Thomas; 1832 list age 72; also 1840 Census; served in N C line; drew pension in Jackson Co; lived with Jesse Jenkins.

Wilkerson, Turner; 1832 list age 76; served in Va line; drew pension in Smith Co.

Wilker, Jacob; 1832 list age 87; served in Pa line; drew pension in Knox Co.

Wilkins, William; 1832 list age 70; served in N C line; drew pension in Lincoln Co.

Wilkinson, William; 1832 list age 72; served in N C line; drew pension in White Co.

Williams, Alexander; 1818 list age 92; served in N C line; drew pension in Hawkins Co; d Oct 8 1830.

Williams, Benjamin; 1832 list age 93; served in Va line; drew pension in Knox Co.

Williams, Capt Beverly; 1840 Census age 57; served in Williamson's mil; drew pension in Gibson Co; (1812).

Williams, Caleb; 1832 list age 73; served in N C mil; drew pension in Stewart Co.

Williams, Capt Daniel; 1828 list; served in 6th N C line; drew pension in Dickson Co.

Williams, David; 1832 list age 79; served in N C line; drew pension in Rutherford Co.

Williams, Elisha; 1840 Census age 80; drew pension in Maury Co.

Williams, Francis; 1832 list age 70; served in Md troops; drew pension in White Co.

Williams, Hickman; 1818 list age 67; served in N C troops; drew pension in Lawrence Co.

Williams, John; 1832 list age 75; also 1840 Census; served in Va line; drew pension in Morgan Co.

Williams, John; 1832 list age 72; also 1840 Census; served in N C line; drew pension in Bedford Co.

Williams, John J; 1832 list age 72; served in N C line; drew pension in Anderson Co.

Williams, Levi; 1832 list age 78; served in Va line; drew pension in Rutherford Co.

Williams, Mathew; 1828 list; served in Williamson's reg't; drew pension in Davidson Co; d Feb 14 1820; (1812).

Williams, Mathias; 1832 list age 78; served in Va line; drew pension in Morgan Co.

Williams Nancy, widow; 1840 Census age 83; drew pension in Wilson Co.

Williams, Robert; 1818 list age 75; served in N C line; drew pension in Davidson Co; d May 28 1826.

Williams, Samuel, Sen; 1832 list age 76; also 1840 Census; served in N C line; drew pension in Wilson Co.

Williams, Shadrach; 1832 list age 72; served in Va line; drew pension in Grainger Co.

Williams, Solomon; 1832 list age 70; served in N C line; drew pension in Fayette Co.

Williams, Thomas; 1840 Census age 79; drew pension in Giles Co.

Williams, Thomas C; 1832 list age 80; served in N C line; drew pension in Wilson Co.

Williams, Tobias; 1832 list age 83; served in N C line; drew pension in Smith Co.

Williams, William; 1832 list age 77; served in Va line; drew pension in Hawkins Co.

Williams, Zebedee; 1818 list; served in N C troops; drew pension in Smith Co.

Williamson, John; 1832 list age 74; also 1840 Census; served in Va mil; drew pension in Davidson Co.

Williamson, John; served in 1st reg't rifles; lived in Cocke Co; d in service Oct 3 1813; his heirs were: Nancy, Elizabeth, Nelson and Reuben Williamson; (1812).

Williamson, Littleton; 1832 list age 74; served in Va line; drew pension in Rutherford Co.

Willie, William; 1840 Census; drew pension in Davidson Co where he lived with Patrick Mynatt.

Williford, Brittain; 1832 list age 93; served in N C line; drew pension in Giles Co.

Williford, Jacob; 1832 list age 78; served in N C line; drew pension in Grainger Co.

Williford, Jordan; 1840 Census age 85; drew pension in Rutherford Co where he lived with Robert Williford.

Willis, Jarvis; 1818 list age 71; served in Md line; drew pension in Franklin Co.

Willis, John; 1832 list age 68; served in N C line; drew pension in Hawkins Co.

Willis, Lewis; 1818 list age 90; served in Va line; drew pension in Greene Co; d Mar 5 1832.

Willis, Meshack; 1818 list; served in Ga troops drew pension in Maury Co.

Willis, Smith; 1832 list age 70; also 1840 Census; served in Pa line; drew pension in 1832 in Morgan Co; drew pension in 1840 in Fentress Co.

Willis, William; 188 list age 74; served in Va line; drew pension in Roane Co.

Wills, David; 1828 list; served in 1st Tenn mil; drew pension in Davidson Co; (1812).

Wills, Thomas C; 1832 list age 69; served in Md line; drew pension in Henry Co.

Wilson, Ann, widow; 1840 Census age 40; drew pension in Franklin Co.

Wilson, James; 1832 list age 76; served in N C line; drew pension in Bedford Co.

Wilson, James; 1840 Census age 86; drew pension in Marshall Co.

Wilson, John; 1832 list age 73; served in N C line; drew pension in Lincoln Co.

Wilson, John; 1832 list age 86; served in N C line; drew pension in Jackson Co.

Wilson, John; 1832 list age 78; served in N C line; drew pension in Carter Co; his widow was Elizabeth Wilson.

Wilson, Joseph; 1832 list age 76; also 1840 Census; served in N C mil; drew pension in 1832 in Carter Co; drew pension in 1840 in Claiborne Co.

Wilson, William; 1832 list age 74; also 1840 Census; served in N C line; drew pension in 1832 in Carter Co; drew pension in 1840 in Johnson Co; lived with William Wilson, Jr.

Winchester, Daniel; 1840 Census age 72; served in N C line; drew pension in Hardin Co.

Winstead, Francis; 1832 list age 81; also 1840 Census; drew pension in Hawkins Co; lived with Margaret Winstead.

Winstead, Nathaniel; 1832 list age 76; also 1840 Census; served in N C line; drew pension in Rutherford Co.

Wise, Peter; 1832 list age 81; also 1840 Census; served in Pa line; drew pension in Cocke Co; lived with Joseph Wise.

Wiser, George; 1832 list age 69; served in Va mil; drew pension in Claiborne Co.

Witcher, James; 1832 list age 82; served in Va line; drew pension in Smith Co.

Witherington, Joseph; 1832 list age 75; also 1840 Census; served in N C line; drew pension in Henry Co.

Witherspoon, John; 1832 list age 71; served in N C line; drew pension in Wayne Co.

Withrow, James; drew pension in Nashville Agency.

Witt, Bergis; 1818 list age 69; also 1840 Census; served in N C line; drew pension in 1818 in McMinn Co; drew pension in 1840 in Monroe Co.

Witt, Miriam Horner, widow of Caleb Witt; applied for pension in Jefferson Co Nov 30 1844.

Wolever, Philip; 1832 list age 83; served in Pa mil; drew pension in Greene Co.

Wollard, John; 1832 list age 74; served in Va line; drew pension in Henry Co.

Wood, Belfield; 1832 list age 80; served in N C mil; drew pension in Franklin Co; d Apr 6 1836; his widow Nancy Kedwell Wood drew pension in 1856; lived in Wayne Co Ky with a son, Belfield Wood.

Wood, Elles; 1840 Census age 87; drew pension in Giles Co; lived with George Erwin.

Wood, John; 1840 Census age 92; drew pension in Jackson Co; lived with Philip Condra.

Wood, John; 1832 list age 72; served in N C line; drew pension in Blount Co.

Wood, John; 1832 list age 82; served in N C line; drew pension in Bedford Co.

Wood, John; 1832 list age 77; served in N C line; drew pension in Bedford Co.

Wood, John; served in 24th reg't inf; lived in Rutherford Co; d in service Oct or Nov 1813; his heirs were: Franklin, John, Lucinda, Jesse, Thomas and Owen; (1812).

Wood, Mathew; 1818 list age 69; served in N C line; drew pension in Giles Co.

Wood, Obadiah; 1832 list age 75; served in N C line; drew pension in Anderson Co.

Wood, Thomas; 1832 list age 91; served in Va mil; drew pension in Wilson Co.

Wood, Zadock; 1832 list age 68; also 1840 Census; served in S C line; drew pension in 1832 in Rutherford Co; drew pension in 1840 in Bedford Co.

Wooddy, John; 1832 list age 77; also 1840 Census; served in N C line; drew pension in Roane Co; in 1840 he lived with Samuel Wooddy.

Woodruff, Benjamin; 1832 list age 73; served in N C line; drew pension in Lincoln Co.

Woodroof, Jesse 1818 list age 71; served in Va troops; drew pension in Lincoln Co.

Woolf, George; 1818 list age 80; served in Pa line; drew pension in Knox Co.

Woosley, Aaron; 1818 list age 81; served in Va troops; drew pension in Lincoln Co.

Wooten, Turner; 1832 list age 77; served in Va line; drew pension in Jefferson Co; d Nov 22 1833.

Wordson, John; 1818 list age 71; served in Va troops; drew pension in Smith Co; d Mar 29 1828.

Workman, Peter; 1818 list age 78; served in N C line; drew pension in Carter Co.

Worley, Zachariah; 1832 list age 72; served in Va line; drew pension in Smith Co.

Wright, William; 1828 list; served in Ramsey's 1st reg't U S inf; drew pension in Knox Co; (1812).

Wyatt, Edward; 1840 Census age 81; drew pension in Roane Co; lived with Daniel White.

Wyley, Alexander; 1832 list age 80; served in N C line; drew pension in Anderson Co.

Wyley, James; 1832 list age 71; served in Va line; drew pension in Blount Co.

Yader (Yoder, Yaden), Joseph; 1832 list age 78; also 1840 Census; served in Va line; drew pension in Grainger Co.

Yager, Solomon, Sen; 1832 list age 75; also 1840 Census; served in Va line; drew pension in White Co.

Yancey, Ambrose; 1832 list age 69; served in Va line; drew pension in Grainger Co.

Yarboro, Davis; 1832 list age 73; served in N C mil; drew pension in Stewart Co.

Yarborough, Henry, Sen; 1832 list age 72; also 1840 Census; served in N C line; drew pension in Tipton Co.

Yates, Samuel; 1832 list age 77; also 1840 Census; served in N C mil; drew pension in Cocke Co.

Yaws, Michael; 1832 list age 82; served in Pa line; drew pension in Hawkins Co.

Yeates, Thomas; 1832 list age 76; served in Pa line; drew pension in Robertson Co.

Young, Archibald; 1832 list age 78; served in Va line; drew pension in Giles Co.

Young, Isham; 1832 list age 74; served in Ga line; drew pension in Roane Co.

Young, Jacob W; 1832 list age 78; also 1840 Census; served in U S Navy on Privateer Defence; drew pension in Maury Co.

Young, Samuel; 1832 list age 78; served in N C line; drew pension in McMinn Co.

Young, William, 3rd; 1832 list age 89; served in N C line; drew pension in Perry Co.

Young, William; 1832 list age 72; served in N C line; drew pension in Henry Co.

Zeck, Jacob; 1832 list age 76; also 1840 Census; served in Pa line; drew pension in Robertson Co.